WHAT WOULD YOGI DO?

Guidelines for Athletes, Coaches, and Parents Who Love Sports

A Hall of Famer's Legacy

by

John D. McCarthy

Foreword by Dale Berra

FIRST EDITION

Hardcover ISBN: 978-0-692-28909-9
eBook ISBN: 978-0-692-29531-1

Cover Design: Stephen Swinton
Edited by: Vivette Watson

Swinton Studio, Inc.
49 New Hampton Road,
Washington, NJ 07882, USA

SwintonStudio.com

Printed in the United States of America

This book is dedicated to

Yogi and **Russ "Pop" Monica**

for their humanity and humility as

athletes, coaches and parents.

Contents

Foreword

By Dale Berra

All my life people have asked me what it's like having an American legend as your dad? I don't see him that way. To me he's just Dad, a regular, down-to-earth person, wonderful family man. As a father, all he ever wanted was to see his kids enjoy whatever they did.

Many people thought I became a major-league player – and that my two other brothers also became professional athletes – because our dad was Yogi Berra. Nothing could be further from the truth. Dad never gave us any instruction, never fussed over our youth or high school games. He just watched quietly, content knowing we were having fun playing sports, trying to be the best we could be.

Obviously sports gave my dad a great life. But nobody worked harder or enjoyed playing more than he did, growing up on the sandlots in St. Louis a long time ago. The lessons he learned were passed on to me and my brothers. You don't need an organized team or adult-supervised practices to get better. And don't just concentrate on one sport. "Play 'em all," he'd say.

When I was in high school in Montclair, NJ, I played football and hockey and baseball. I loved the different seasons, the different skills, the different teammates. When scouts told me I had a chance to be a No. 1 draft pick in the major-league draft (which I became in 1975), I was advised to quit the other sports to not risk getting injured. Dad just balked. "Keep playing if you want to. Whatever happens will happen. If you love playing, keep playing."

As a father, as a Hall of Fame catcher, and later as a coach and manager, Dad always kept it simple. And that to me is the essence of his genius. For a man without a formal education, he was, as Craig Biggio once said, "the smartest man I ever met in baseball." The impact he had on others – his teammates, the players he mentored – is remarkable. Don Mattingly, whom Dad encouraged early in his career with the Yankees, now wears No. 8 as Dodgers manager, a tribute to what he meant to him.

What always meant most to Dad was doing things right – to be honest, to play fair, to respect the game. That's the theme of all the programs at the Yogi Berra Museum (YBM) & Learning Center. Sports teach a lot about ourselves – discipline, teamwork, perseverance. And like I said, nobody got more out of sports than Dad. On and off the playing field, he always made good choices. Through sports, he developed an unimaginable number of friendships and has lived a long, wonderful and successful life.

Without question the world is more complex than when Dad grew up – and even when I was a kid in the 1960's. Youth sports have essentially become professionalized, with personal instructors, expensive club and travel teams, you name it. And professional sports have gotten endlessly complicated, too, with video and analysis and statistics on everything.

But sports are still sports. As Dad always said, someone's got to win, someone's got to lose. If you lose, give the other guy his due, and try harder next time. It sounds simple, but as an athlete, a father and coach and manager, my Dad's always been unique. And inspiring. In terms of accomplishment and character, I believe each of us can learn a great deal from Yogi Berra.

I'm glad that John has written a book that reveals my Dad's view of how athletes, coaches, and especially parents should view sports. That, I believe, is his true legacy.

Introduction

What's in a Name?

Located on the northern most point of the campus of Montclair State University, in Little Falls, NJ is a one-story edifice visited by thousands each year. Many are locals, but some have come from as far away as Alaska. Each visitor has his own reason for coming to the Yogi Berra Museum and Learning Center. Many are long-time Yankee fans. Many are seniors in search of a memento or two which will spark a memory of the glorious days of the 50's and 60's, when the Bronx Bombers ruled the national pastime. They fondly remember the lovable, feisty, talented player who squatted behind home plate, who led the Yanks to five consecutive World Series titles, picking up three MVP Awards along the way. Many visitors never saw him play. Their only connection to him is as a pitchman for Yoo-Hoo, or AFLAC.

Once inside, they stand at the case which displays his 10 World Series rings, a feat that no one else who ever wore a major league uniform has accomplished. They move along to his three MVP plaques, a life-sized photo of him with Babe Ruth and a video loop of the numerous TV cameos and commercials in which he appeared. If they are truly observant, however, they will notice that most of the displays are photos of Yogi with Carmen, his wife of 65 years, along with their three sons, Larry, Timmy, and Dale, their wives, and Yogi's 11 grandchildren.

The Museum, appropriately situated adjacent to a minor league baseball stadium, is much more than a collection of artifacts. It's a place where hundreds of elementary school children disembark long, yellow buses, and enter wide-eyed, to learn about an individual who came from a modest, uneducated family in St. Louis, a man who, despite obvious physical limitations, used baseball as a vehicle to become an

American icon. It's a place where inner-city youth come to baseball and softball camps every summer, where aspiring broadcasters come to learn the tricks of the trade from veteran sportscasters Bruce Beck (NBC) and Ian Eagle (CBS), and high school athletes come to learn about sportsmanship and being the best teammate at the Institute for Coaching.

The lettering on the outside of the building, billing it as The Yogi Berra Museum & Learning Center, is significant and was carefully chosen. The memorabilia it houses is only a small, though impressive, part of its mission. In 2005, along with museum director, Dave Kaplan, and Dr. Rob Gilbert, author and professor of sports psychology at MSU, I helped found the Institute of Coaching and Center for Sports Parenting at the Museum. Since then, Dr. Gilbert and I have given over 500 talks to high school athletes, coaches, and parents. Our focus is always the same, whether we meet them in small groups in the theater in the Museum, or in large auditoriums throughout the state: There is much we can gain through participation in sports, if we learn to compete with character. That's not our message; we just deliver it. It belongs to Yogi, and that is really his legacy.

Behind the witty sayings–"Yogisms" as they are known–is a profoundly decent man who is deeply respected by those who know him, not only for his Hall of Fame accomplishments, but for the quality of life he lived. As much as he has received, he has given more. His work ethic, love of family, concern for the well-being of others, generosity, wit and sense of fair play make Yogi an ideal role model. There isn't a person on the planet who doesn't smile at the mere mention of his name.

Numerous books have been written about Yogi's life and exploits on the field. The purpose of this book is not to recount Yogi's playing career. Rather the goal is to provide specific guidelines for athletes, coaches, and parents, which emanate from Yogi's core beliefs - beliefs that grew out of a time when we weren't reading about showboating, pampered athletes, abusive, unethical coaches, and overzealous, over-indulgent parents - so that the benefits of amateur sports can be maximized.

We can't change today's culture, its pace too fast, its reach too global. However, we can and must change the culture of sports, at least on the amateur level. To do so will require cooperation among athletes, coaches, and parents. This book, divided into three sections, is filled with specific suggestions for each part of the sports triumvirate to get us back on track. It is not meant to be read selectively by section, but rather in total, so that everyone has the same information. For too long athletes, coaches, and parents have been spoken to, or targeted in writing, as separate entities. My goal is to get them on the same page, literally. By pointing out common threads running through their respective experiences, my hope is that everyone will have a better understanding of the necessary alliances that need to be formed. It strikes me that relationships among the three parties have become increasingly adversarial, so much so that many coaches, good ones, are walking away from the profession they once cherished because they don't feel it's worth the hassle. Playing time, once regarded as something to be earned, has come to be regarded as an entitlement, and the battle lines have been drawn. We've lost the sense that we're all in this together. The outcome has become much more important than the process. External forces–the skyrocketing cost of a college education, the saturation of sports on TV, sports talk radio and internet blogs, and social media - have eroded the once highly respected relationship between an athlete, his/her coach, and his/her parents. That distresses Yogi, and it distresses me as well. That's why I wrote this book.

It's not too late to turn back the clock to the days Yogi knew, when sports done the right way made us better people. If the programs offered at the Museum, which are the basis for the content of these pages, help restore integrity in sports, Yogi's legacy will endure.

COMMON GROUND

HOW TO GET THE MOST OUT OF SPORTS
FOR EVERYONE INVOLVED

Athletes, Coaches and Parents

HOW DO WE REACH COMMON GROUND?

We need to stop the self-fulfilling
prophecy that it's getting worse.

We need to change our focus from
winning to competing.

We need to stop enabling our kids and
start empowering them.

We need athletes, coaches and parents
who are willing to:

**Listen, Trust, Empower,
Communicate, Support and Model.**

ATHLETES

You made the choice to participate on the team; make the most of it, and you'll have memories for a lifetime.

FACT: The only post-season award everyone on the team has the same chance to earn is BEST TEAMMATE.

FACT: The only one who can stop you from reaching your potential is you.

What athletes can do:

Listen. Try not to take constructive criticism from coaches personally. Respond to the coaches' suggestions with a change in your actions or your attitude. The only voice that matters during a game belongs to your coach, so tune everyone else out. Keep your eyes out of the stands and your head in the game. To be successful in any endeavor, you must be focused. Listen and learn.

Trust. Your coaches are experienced and are students of your sport. They usually have playing experience and have attended coaching clinics to enhance their knowledge. Give them the chance to prove that they know what's best for the team. Have faith that responding to your coaches' instruction and working hard will help you improve.

Empower. Respect your captains. Handle all in-fighting and resolve conflicts before the coach has to get involved. Take responsibility for all of your actions. If you make a mistake, own up to it. You are a young adult now, so act like one.

Communicate. Tell your parents that you appreciate their support, but you don't want them to talk to your coaches about your playing situation. Don't let something fester inside of you. If you have an issue with another player or a coach, pick an appropriate time and honestly express your feelings. Don't hurt the chemistry of your team by pouting or carrying a grudge.

Support. Try to interact with everyone on the team, not just the stars, your friends, or your classmates. If you are a starter, be sure to encourage the substitutes. If you are on the varsity, spend time watching the freshmen and the junior varsity teams compete. Remember what it was like when you played on that level. Be sure you know all the plays, strategies, etc., so that your teammates and coaches can be sure you can be counted on at any moment. Your goal should be to be regarded as the best teammate. The expression "You can't rock the boat if you're too busy rowing" is especially true in sports. Teams succeed when everyone cares, and everyone knows everyone cares.

Model. You represent your family and your school. Don't embarrass them by losing self-control. Never talk to an official or to an opponent disrespectfully. Carry yourself with class at all times and you'll never have to apologize. Make it very clear to your teammates that you will neither participate in nor tolerate any form of hazing. No one has the right to belittle another human being, and no team has the right to tarnish the reputation of the school.

Tom Seaver and Yogi celebrate winning the 1973 National League pennant, a season which spawned the famous Yogi-ism, "It ain't over til it's over."

As a manager in 1964, Yogi was not averse to throwing batting practice. In 1976, he rejoined the Yankees and became the first bench coach in baseball.

COACHES

Next to their parents, a coach often plays the most dominant role in a young athlete's life.

FACT: You are a teacher, first and foremost. You must always place your players' physical and mental well-being above all else.

FACT: For the overwhelming majority of your players, this will be the last opportunity they have to participate in an organized, competitive sport.

What coaches can do:

Listen. Try not to be close-minded. Be responsive to suggestions from your assistants, your AD, players, and clinicians. Encourage athletes to come to you to discuss their concerns. If you sense that an athlete might have an issue but seems hesitant to talk to you, initiate the conversation. From day one your players should know that you are there for them.

Trust. Once you have made decisions after careful planning, stick to them. Trust your ability to coach smart and exude confidence in yourself and your program. This doesn't mean you project a "my way or the highway" persona. It simply means to have faith in yourself.

Empower. Let your assistants coach. Don't micro-manage. Select captains and give them meaningful responsibilities. You only need one rule: "To play for our school, players need to be in the right place, at the right time, and do the right thing." Let your players ask themselves, "Am I doing the right thing now?" If you tell them what to do all of the time, how will they learn? Remember, you are a teacher.

Communicate. Let your players know exactly what you expect of them at your first pre-season meeting. The same goes for assistants. Inform parents of your practice schedule for the season. Avoid surprises. Respond to e-mails the day you get them. Keep your AD in the loop. If players need to be cut, do it in person, not by posting a "cut list". It's difficult for everyone, especially teenagers, to deal with rejection. Explain *why* you had to let the player go. If not, you'll probably have to tell the parents or the principal the next day.

Support. All people respond to praise. <u>Never</u> publicly embarrass a player. Coach every kid, not just the starters. Create opportunities for all athletes to compete. (e.g., sophomore games, novice track meets, etc.) Avoid pressuring an athlete to stick to one sport. It's his/her choice, not yours. Encourage your team to attend other teams' games at your school whenever they can. Most importantly, allow students time to get extra help from teachers, even if it means that he/she is late to practice.

Model. Keep your emotions in check. You can't expect players and parents to display sportsmanship if you don't. Remember that at all times, you represent the school district. When the game is on the line, you need to be the calmest individual in the gym or on the field. Don't punish your team, with a penalty or a technical foul, because you lost your composure.

Dale Berra with his dad when Yogi managed the Yankees in the mid 1980's.
A nice father-son reunion, but no special favors.

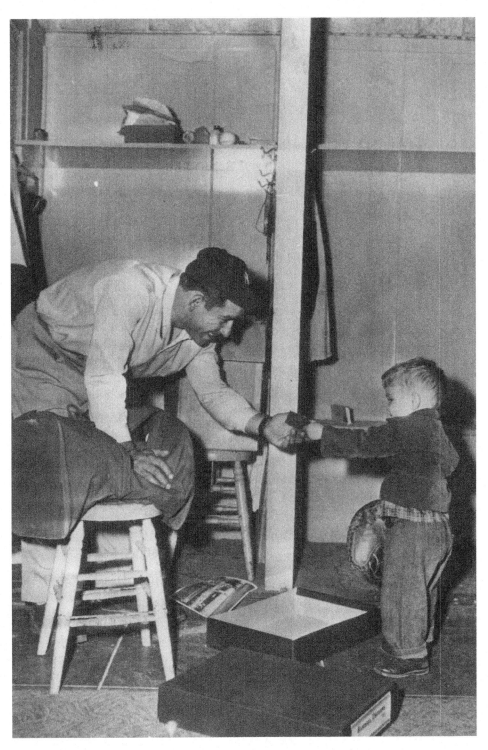

Yogi gets an assist from his first-born son, Larry, as he cleans out his locker.
Originally from St. Louis, Yogi and his wife Carmen raised their three sons in Montclair, NJ.

PARENTS

You are your child's first teacher, best teacher, and lifelong teacher.

FACT: Seeking approval, children model their parents' behavior- the good and the bad.

FACT: Despite what is written about peer pressure, parents maintain the most influence over their children's attitudes concerning competition and sportsmanship.

What parents can do:

Listen. Let him/her vent. They just want someone to listen. Try to resist giving advice unless you are asked for it. Refrain from relating your experiences as an athlete.

Trust. Give your child over to the coach. You may disagree with the coach, but try to trust that the coach is knowledgeable and fair-minded. Don't coach from the stands. Players need to hear only one voice—the coach's.

Empower. Try not to intercede for your child. If he/she has a problem with a coach or a teacher, you might suggest ways he/she might handle the situation, but let him/her work it out. This is a major component of personal growth. Soon he/she will be away at college and faced with many decisions. How can one make good choices without prior practice?

Communicate. If you have information the coach should know about your child (health, family situation, etc.), write a personal note or send an e-mail. Don't send plays to the coach that you know will work. If you have an issue with a coach, write an e-mail, wait 24 hours, then send it. If you don't get a timely response, contact the AD.

Support. Root for everyone on the team, not just your son/daughter. It's more fun, and eases your personal angst. Volunteer to help at the games. Avoid second-guessing the coach (it's harder to make the first decision), and limit the PGA (post game analysis) at home. Be thankful for your youngster's opportunity to compete and have fun.

Model. Your child takes cues from you. If you want your youngster to display sportsmanship, you must model it yourself. There's no place for berating officials, coaches, or players in sports, especially youth sports. If you feel yourself losing control, go for a walk and return when you are calmer. You'd be surprised at the number of athletes who confess that they are distracted and/or embarrassed by their parents' behavior at their games.

SHARED VISION

Athletes, Coaches, and Parents need to recognize that for sports to thrive, their focus should be on competing, not winning. Each group must share the same vision, or the culture of sports will fulfill the prophecy of cynics.

This "Shared Vision" is not just a catch phrase that Yogi would espouse; it is a reflection of how he has lived his life as an athlete, coach and parent. When you're faced with decisions regarding athletic competition, you can follow Yogi's lead. When you examine, what Yogi did, you'll know, "What Would Yogi Do?" were he in your position.

As an athlete, Yogi listened to his coaches and trusted their advice. He worked hard at improving his weaknesses as a catcher and never blamed anyone for his failings. He communicated with his teammates and always supported them. He even gave up his position and moved to the outfield so the manager could add another bat to the lineup. His goal was always to be considered the best teammate. He was, and is, considered a model Yankee.

As a coach, Yogi listened to his assistants and trusted their input. When his teams lost, he never blamed the players or the umpires. His door was always open to his players and the press. As manager of the Mets he held off the press after a slow start. He called for everyone to be patient in their support of the team and guaranteed that in time the players would turn things around. He was spot on. The Mets went on to win the pennant. Coaches would do well to model themselves after Yogi. He was a players-first coach, who is revered by the men who played under him for the Yankees, Mets, and Astros. They show that respect by returning yearly from distant parts of the country to his annual golf outing.

As a parent, Yogi listened to his sons when it came to the sports they wanted to play. He trusted their judgment, and never suggested that they follow in his footsteps. He encouraged them to play more than one sport and once fended off a scout who tried to get one of his sons to stop playing high school hockey saying, "I had my shot. He can decide for himself what he wants to do." Yogi didn't attend all of their games because his schedule wouldn't allow it. However, he fully supported them, whether it was driving up to UMass to see Tim play football, travelling to a spring training site to watch Larry get his first minor league hit off of Ron Guidry, or coaching Dale during his stint with the Yankees. Most of his communication with his sons took place on the golf course. He never spoke to any of their coaches or criticized how they were being coached. In that respect he is an exception to many adults who today are engaged in behaviors that are tilting the focus to the bleachers instead of the fields and courts, where it belongs. As hard as it might be to stand back and let young athletes find their way in the changing sports landscape, parents would do well to model themselves after Yogi, who would tell them, "We had our shot. Now it's their turn."

Part I - Athletes

"Baseball is 90% mental.
The other half is physical"
- Yogi Berra

The most important question for an athlete: Are you going to go all out or hold back?

Being part of a team is a wonderful experience. You get a sense of belonging, of being part of something bigger than yourself. For some, that feeling is enough, and there is nothing wrong with that. However, some athletes want more. They want a feeling of accomplishment. The question then becomes: How hard are you willing to work to get what you want? It's the same way with school. Do you want A's in your classes? Do you pay attention in class? Take detailed notes? Ask questions? Study every night? Seek extra help? Participate in study groups? Or do you just want A's, but work at a B/C level? The point is, being good at something – school or sports – requires hard work.

Much has been written about talent, and the overwhelming consensus is that no one is born with it. Not Mozart, not Michelangelo, not Tiger Woods, Serena Williams or LeBron James. Don't believe me? Read the research presented in *The Talent Code* by Daniel Coyle. Everyone who has mastered a skill has spent roughly 10,000 hours of deliberate practice. The best athletes, regardless of their sport, are always the hardest workers. What sets them apart is that once they achieve some success, they never stop working. Don't believe me? Google Jerry Rice's off-season workout. Rice was lightly recruited out of high school. He went to a small college, and was drafted in a low round. He went on to become the all-time leading pass receiver in the NFL, a perennial All-pro, and multiple Super Bowl champion. He is regarded by many as possibly the best NFL player ever. Was he the most talented? Apparently college coaches and NFL scouts didn't think so. Was he the hardest worker? Watch his workout video and decide for yourself.

My experience as a high school and college coach (basketball, baseball, football, and soccer) is more anecdotal than scientific, but my best players were always the hardest workers, by far. They came early to practice and stayed late. They played multiple sports, and worked on their game over the summer. They took my suggestions as helpful tips, not criticisms.

Not every athlete is willing to put the time in to reach his/her potential. That's a choice, and that's fine. However, there are consequences, as one of my basketball players, Glenn, found out. At the end of each season, I met with underclassmen to review their season and tell them what they needed to work on over the summer. After Glenn's junior season, I told him that we face mostly zone defenses, and as a 2 guard he needed to be able to consistently make a wing jump shot (better than 45%). I suggested that he take 200 jumpers from each wing as often as possible—not just 400 shots, one shot done correctly 400 times—and keep a chart of his results. He agreed that was a good plan. Summer came. Glenn got a new Mustang convertible, met Barbara, and spent his time cruising down the shore with his new girl. Who could blame him? Cool car, great girlfriend. You know where this is going. Glenn didn't shoot 400 shots the entire summer. When the basketball season came, Glenn had a great seat for all the action, right next to me. He played some, but not nearly enough for him, or his parents to be happy. It wasn't a punishment. He made a choice, probably a good one for him, and as his coach, so did I.

So again I ask: How hard are you willing to work to get what you want out of your sport? Will the work guarantee you a starting role? An all-conference selection? No, but a lack of work will guarantee you a seat next to your coach. Are you willing to go "all out" and risk everything, or will you hold back and gain nothing? The best athletes always go "all out" and live with the results. The safe road is to just say, "I could have made it (starting role, starring role), but I didn't really want it." Which road do you think Tiger, LeBron, Serena and other top college and pro athletes took? Which one will you take?

Discussing the Triple Play Series of presentations with Museum Director Dave Kaplan.

Evan's Story

At the age of five, Evan knew he wanted to be a dancer. After a tee ball game one Saturday, his mother picked him up and drove to pick up Evan's sister from her dance class. Peering into the room, Evan saw everyone smiling and having fun, more fun than tee ball anyway. He stayed with baseball but asked his mother if he could take dance lessons as well. He worked hard at it and began to see results. The harder he worked, the better he got. In fact, he started getting lead roles in dance recitals! At one point, he was asked to audition for a spot on a dance tour group. He was told he couldn't miss any rehearsals or he'd be dropped. This created a conflict since he continued playing baseball, a sport in which his father had excelled. (His father was drafted by the Cincinnati Reds.) One day, during an at bat, Evan realized that he might miss a rehearsal if he continued playing. He dropped the bat, turned to the ump and said, "Sorry, I gotta go. I have dance practice." What former major league draftee doesn't live to hear his son say those words? Evan's dad simply said to a friend sitting next to him, "That's my boy!"

Evan made it to rehearsal, and many more after that. He went on to dance in numerous recitals, including one in Lincoln Center. He expanded his interest to include tap dancing and singing. This led to his appearance in several plays and eventually settled his mind on a college major. He chose to become a Theater Arts major at Montclair State University. Having practiced tap dancing four times a week, two hours a day, for over a decade, he was ready to make his mark as America's next tap dancing sensation.

Unfortunately, fate and bad luck had other plans. After experiencing discomfort in his lower leg, Evan was told he needed surgery. It was then discovered that Evan had bone cancer. Several operations later, it was determined that the leg, from the knee down, would need to be amputated in order to save his life. He was 19 at the time.

Things got even worse for Evan. The cancer spread to his lungs. Sixteen rounds of chemotherapy were required. Hair loss and severe mouth sores ensued. Through it all, Evan told his doctors that he would dance again. Inspired by Peg-leg Joe, a one-legged tap dancer who appeared on a popular TV show in the 60's, Evan requested a peg leg in addition to a conventional prosthetic leg. True to his word, Evan returned to MSU, and even more remarkably, returned to tap dancing. He appeared in shows and performed in recitals. He also made an appearance on "American Idol." Videos of him performing went viral. (Google Evan Ruggiero – one-legged dancer.) He was interviewed on "Inside Edition" and appeared on "The Ellen Show."

I'm telling you Evan's story for several reasons. First, he is the most inspiring individual I know personally. Secondly, he is the best example of going "All Out" I can share with you. He wasn't born talented, and when it was taken from him, he refused to let it go. Evan now works with Dr. Gilbert and me at the Yogi Berra Museum. He instantly connects with our high school guests; they all want their picture taken with him. He embodies everything we want to convey to young people, and everything that Yogi represents: Anything worth doing is worth doing well; whatever we do should inspire others to work hard.

Evan also helps us make another point about what we can learn from sports, namely, how do we handle success and setbacks? As Bob Hurley, Hall of Fame basketball coach from St. Anthony's in Jersey City, NJ, once remarked, "Nobody gets through life undefeated. We all have to deal with adversity." Evan has had more than his share of setbacks, and he is on his way to certain stardom. He displayed what we refer to in our talks with athletes as "Bounce Back Ability" (more specifics on this later). As mentioned earlier, when you go "All Out" there's a risk that things won't always go your way. Aiming high will do that. The question then is: How will you handle success and, more importantly, how will you handle failure?

One thing that Evan shares with Yogi – they have no ego. You'll never hear them brag about something they did. They're modest to a fault, and like Jerry Rice, once they experienced success, they worked even harder to maintain it. As for handling failure? Evan didn't get every part he auditioned for and didn't make it to Hollywood on "American Idol" (He was robbed!). Nothing deters him. He keeps working. Similarly, when Yogi came to the majors, he was a good hitter, but a poor fielding catcher. He spent countless hours being mentored by Bill Dickey during spring training trying to improve. It took years until he was considered an all-around All-Star, and one of the top 50 players of all time. Evan Ruggiero and Yogi Berra are definitely in my "Going All Out" Hall of Fame. You would do well to follow their lead.

Athletes

Are you willing to go all out? When you encounter a setback, will you see it as a problem or a challenge? If you give up on yourself, everyone else will.

Evan Ruggiero

The Player's Dozen

There are sacrifices that as an athlete you have to be willing to make. You need to remain positive and focused, no matter what happens. You must consider the team's needs over your personal goals. You must often act differently than you feel. Your coach will ask you to:

1. Keep your academic house in order.

- You can't play if your grades are inferior, and you certainly won't get recruited.

- One percent of high school athletes will make it to the professional level. Your grades should be your first priority.

- It's better to miss practice than to fail because you didn't get extra help.

Don't wait until your junior or senior year to start focusing on your grades. By then it will be too late. You alone are responsible for performing in the classroom. Sit up front, take notes, ask questions and get extra help if you need it. Try to develop a personal relationship with as many teachers as you can. You will need three strong recommendations when you apply to college. You need to bring the same energy to your studies that you bring to your sport. Far too many stellar athletes don't play in college because they don't qualify academically. Don't let that happen to you.

2. Keep your body strong and healthy.

- **NO CHEATING!** No steroids, no alcohol, no marijuana, no cigarettes.

- Come out for the team already in shape—
don't rely on your coach to condition you.

- Be sure to get enough sleep—
the best hours are before midnight.

It's much easier to get into shape for a season if you maintain some type of conditioning throughout the year. The best way to do this is to play multiple sports, especially until your junior or senior year. Playing more than one sport gives you more opportunities to compete and broadens your exposure to a variety of coaching and motivational styles. Specialization has merits, but only for elite athletes. The easiest way to determine whether or not you are an "elite" athlete is by honestly looking at which schools are recruiting you. There are no secrets on the Division 1 level, and most college recruiters contact prospects early in their high school career.

3. Keep your disciplinary record clean.

- College coaches don't want a kid who's a problem, regardless of his/her talent.

- Keep an eye on your teammates, especially those who have been in trouble in the past—make sure they know that you need them. Suspended players can't help a team.

There's a saying among college recruiters that "Nobody wants to dance with somebody else's devil." College coaches don't want to spend time disciplining players. They would rather take a player with a lesser talent than someone who will bring negative publicity to their school. Recruiters will go so far as to question a school custodian about a potential recruit's character. They can't afford to make a mistake on a kid. Their livelihood depends on their ability to recommend players to their head coach who will add, not detract, from their program. Any hint of drug or alcohol abuse or suspensions is a deal breaker.

4. Keep your school's reputation in mind.

- Try to ensure there are no DQ's (disqualifications)— keep players away from officials.

- Guarantee your coach that there will be no hazing on your watch. No one has the right to spoil a school's reputation. Many people worked hard to establish it.

While much of it goes unreported, 30% of high schools experience some form of hazing each year. The most successful teams are the ones where everyone feels part of the overall mission. Negatively singling out individuals because they're underclassmen or lack ability is a contradiction of a team concept, where we are ALL in this together. The name on the front of your uniform is what matters. It takes decades to build a good reputation and only one stupid, selfish, immature act of bullying or hazing to tarnish it. You have an individual responsibility to your coach and to your school to make sure nothing occurs on your watch. You wouldn't want to be taunted, so don't let it happen to anyone on your team.

5. Keep sports in perspective.

- It's about building relationships and having fun.

- Sports impact on you; they don't define you.

- There's $1 billion available in athletic scholarships per year; there's $22 billion in academic scholarships.

When you are involved in any activity, especially a sport, you generally experience tunnel vision. It's as if this is the only thing that matters. That's only natural. As you get older, you'll realize that what you'll value most are not the wins and titles but the relationships you developed with your teammates and your coaches. If you are talented enough, and lucky enough, to play a sport in college, all the games you play in will pale in comparison to how you will feel

28

with your diploma in hand being congratulated by your family. If you doubt, this, Google any college graduation ceremony and check out the faces of the graduates.

6. Keep in mind that it's about relationships, not rules.

- To be successful, you need to follow only one rule: Be at the right place, at the right time, and do the right thing.

- At the end of the season, regardless of the record, will you be glad that it's over, or sad that it's over? How you make your teammates feel will determine that for you.

Make it a habit to not only be on time, but to be early. It shows that you are ready and willing to be committed to something larger than yourself. When Coach K took over the Dream Team in the Olympics, the very first thing he asked of the players selected was that they be on time for practice. From the best basketball players in the world, he wanted that? Yes. He felt that if they couldn't commit to that, they wouldn't commit to sharing the ball and playing defense. The players agreed; we've seen the results. Will you be early? Will you do what you know in your heart is the right thing when faced with difficult choices, or will you be paralyzed by WWOPT (What Will Other People Think)? Here's a suggestion: When you're faced with a situation calling for you to do the right thing, pretend your grandmother is standing next to you. You'll know what to do.

7. Be personally accountable.

- Leadership is action, not position, or title.

- Be the first one in the locker room and the last to leave.

- All eyes are on you. You get NO DAYS OFF!
  If you make a mistake, admit it.

- Be a thermostat, not a thermometer.
  The first sets the climate, the latter only measures it.

Once you decide to participate in a sport, your life becomes more public. Like it or not, people will be judging the way you act all of the time. On the positive side, you will be noticed by more people, and you will have opportunities to demonstrate your passion, skill and willingness to take risks. On the negative side, your character will always be up for evaluation. The good thing is, you can control how you are viewed. Are you a leader? Act like one. Are you a team player? Show it. When you make a mistake, admit it and own it. If you want people to see you as a person they can trust, give them proof.

8. Insulate your coaches.

- Handle internal conflicts—
  call a team meeting if you feel it's necessary.

- "Step up" when there's a problem.
  Don't be afraid of WWOPS (what will other people say).
  Let coaches handle the preparation;
  you handle the motivation.

For a team to be successful, coaches need to spend their time teaching fundamentals, scouting opponents, reviewing tapes and planning for practices and games. They can't be distracted by any petty jealousies or in-team conflict. Team chemistry is important from Pee Wee to the Pros. Ask yourself: Am I a "Builder Upper" or a "Tearer Downer"? "Do I make a positive contribution to my team, or am I a source of negativity? Do I quickly respond to being coached, or do I gripe about playing time, etc.?" If you aren't happy being on the team, don't show it. Suck it up until the season ends, and don't tryout the following year. Coaches aren't always right, but they're still in control. Accept their decisions, and make the best of it. It will serve you well in the long run.

9. Factor your parents out.

- You're a young adult—act like it. If you have a problem with a coach or a teacher, speak with that person. Don't have your parents call for you.

- Tell your parents that you want to handle your own issues, including your playing time.

Your parents want what is best for you. Sometimes this causes them to want to intervene with your teachers and coaches on your behalf. It's hard being a parent, and even harder to be a parent of an athlete. You can help take some of the pressure off of them by becoming your own advocate. If you have a problem in school or on your team, make an appointment to speak with your teacher or coach. Your parents can help by suggesting questions you might ask. Tell them you are capable of "fighting your own battles," so to speak. In the end, you may not get exactly what you want, but your teacher and coach will have more respect for you. Trust me on that one. I taught for 40 years and coached for 25, and parental interference never ends well.

10. Interact with everyone on the team.

- Remember: T.E.A.M.—
  Together Everyone Achieves More.

- Socialize, don't ostracize.
  Team chemistry is a great equalizer.

- Remember: A candle loses nothing by lighting another.

It's not always possible to be liked by everyone, but it is possible to be respected. The best way to earn respect is to treat everyone the way you want to be treated. Display a team-first attitude and accept your role on the team, regardless of whether you are a starter or rarely play. You can do this by continually encouraging other players' efforts. Be a "high-fiver." No player should be above getting other players water or carrying the equipment. It requires mental toughness to do these things when you don't play as much as you'd like, but that's what being on a team is all about. Everyone respects a team player. When the best players are also the best teammates, like Yogi, good things happen.

11. Remember: It's players who win or lose, not coaches.

- Teams win in spite of poor coaching and lose despite great coaches.

- As John Wooden said, "You are totally in control of your success, not the coach, the ref, or the opponent."

- As legendary football coach, Amos Alonzo Stagg said, "No coach ever won a game by what he knew; it's what his players have learned."

Coaches always get too much credit for success and too much blame for failure. We often hear them say, "I don't tackle, etc., the players do" or "I didn't make one basket this season, the players did." These seem like empty words, but they are 100% accurate. No team wins without talented athletes who work hard. Coaches can't magically 'will' untalented players to perform at a championship level. It takes a group of skilled athletes willing to give 100% everyday to achieve success. Most coaches work very hard and are committed to fielding a winning team. When things go wrong, it's easy to blame the coach. Instead, ask yourself: Am I doing everything possible for my team? Encourage your teammates to do the same. Players win and lose games, not coaches.

12. Set one goal: To be the best teammate.

- Not everyone can be the MVP of the team, but all team members have an equal chance at being regarded as the best teammate.

- "It's about we, not me."

- A dream without a team is a nightmare.

With each season comes a new sense of optimism. Every team starts with the same 0-0 record. Before long it becomes apparent to everyone, players, coaches, parents, and fans, who the best players ON the team are. They're usually the ones with the best statistics and the most press clippings. What's harder to determine is who are the best players FOR the team. Whose efforts make everyone better? Whose individual sacrifices and behaviors create a winning culture? Whether or not your coach or AD recognizes the Best Teammate with an award, everyone knows who that person is and really values him/her. Why not try to be that person? You don't have to be the most talented athlete. You simply have to demonstrate that you always put the team first and fully embrace your role, whether you play the most or the least number of minutes. An MVP award is great – it reflects the quality of one's performance. A Best Teammate Award designation is even better – it reflects the quality of one's character.

Long after your playing days are over, unless you were on an undefeated team, you probably won't remember your seasonal records. Even if you can, will anyone else care? What you will remember, however, are the individuals who were your best teammates. In some instances, you may even be able to trace how their influence impacted you later on in your life. You probably won't recall what they said, but you'll never forget how they made you feel. I was fortunate to play with a number of great teammates, especially Matty Sellitto.

Matty was a senior offensive lineman on our championship team when I was a sophomore. He was the captain; I rarely played, except on special teams. Matty didn't care whether you were the starting QB or the last man on the team. He treated everyone the same way. Instead of leading the team out of the locker room to the cheering of the crowd on game day, he waited by the door and patted every player on the helmet or the shoulder pads. He was the same at practice. As sophomores, we were generally responsible for lugging the blocking and tackling dummies into the field house at the end of practice. Most of the time, Matty walked along side us, or carried some equipment, to show us that we were all on the same team.

Matty knew the secret. He knew that teams thrived when everyone felt included. He knew that Together Everyone Achieves More (T.E.A.M.). To him, this wasn't a catch phrase. He lived it. His team was particularly good on defense so he came up with a unique way of keeping everyone focused on their reliance on defense to win games. He purchased a small, rubber, monster-like figure and taped it to the door leading to the exit from our locker room. Matty stood next to it and made sure that every player on the team touched the "monster" ("monster" was one of our defensive signal calls) on the way out. He watched all 50 plus guys pat the figure he had strategically placed. Some of these guys never played a down! Matty didn't care. To him, they were part of his team.

I mentioned that his team won the state title, but the season wasn't without some troublesome days. One in particular, remains with me still. It was mid-way through the season, on an unseasonably warm October afternoon when a parish priest showed up to talk to our head coach just as we were completing a two-hour practice. Though they spoke off to the side, we knew something bad was brewing. Father Otto informed our coach that over the previous weekend a few football players attended a party hosted by a girl who was baby-sitting for a neighbor. The house was trashed; the owners were considering pressing charges. Without an explanation, our coach came over to us, told one of the assistants to "Put them through the paces," and walked away.

"Everybody on the goal line. Drop on all fours and on my whistle start crawling to the opposite goal line," barked the assistant coach. We could hear his anger in the piercing sound of the whistle, and off we went, 100 yards on all fours! "On your feet; jog back to the other goal line." The dust from our grassless field started to settle on our mouthpieces. "Now drop to your knees and crawl those same hundred yards." Down we went. Over the course of the two additional trips, a number of guys began to hurl their lunch. I was lightheaded and exhausted, ready to quit. One by one, guys tried to lie down and give up. They were all met by Matty's voice. "Get up. Don't you quit. We're all part of this team. Keep moving." And so we did, because it was Matty. The guy who had always included us. Even though the majority of us had not brought this punishment on, we endured it because we were part of the team, Matty's team. When it was over, we were silent as we limped to the field house, all 50 plus guys. We had survived and were ready to move on.

So why am I telling you this? Do I think being "Put through the paces" was justified? No. I think the assistant coach was lucky that no one was seriously injured. I'm telling you this story, just as I tell all the students who come to our athletes seminar at the YBM so they will understand that inclusion is the key to effective leadership, and that "It's about others" isn't just a slogan. It's the DNA of a great teammate.

Like everyone else, you will encounter some troublesome days in your life. Many times they'll come with little or no warning and will be life-altering. They will certainly test your mettle. I know this first-hand. Two years after being diagnosed with breast cancer, my wife died, leaving me to raise our 13 year old daughter. It had been an emotionally draining two years watching Pam courageously battle the disease. We had been together since high school, almost 30 years. I can tell you that it was a real struggle to move on. When people asked, "Where did you find the stamina to show up every day and do your job while raising a 13-year-old daughter all by yourself?" My response was always the same – just two words: "Matty Sellitto." They probably didn't understand. I hope you do.

ATHLETES

Fully accept Coach John Wooden's reminder to his players: "You are totally in control of your success, not the coach, the ref, or the opponent. The only way to get better is to work harder and smarter."

Another congratulatory talk to the Montclair H.S. Football Team. The Mounties won back-to-back state titles. They had great talent and outstanding coaches.

Things I Wish I Had Known as an Athlete

Will beats Skill

While it's true that the teams with the most talented players win most of their games, it is also true that hard work beats talent when talent doesn't work hard. The thing I learned about talent is that it's overrated and misunderstood. Do you really think that people are born talented? LeBron was dunking the ball in the hospital nursery? Tiger was draining putts in his playpen? Jay Z's first words were in the form of a rap? You know better than that. Unfortunately, I didn't. Which, as I look back on it, was a blessing.

I had always thought guys were lucky to be born strong, to have such a great shooting eye, or a smooth batting stroke. That made me work even harder to catch up. I played sports from sun up until sun down every day I wasn't in school. The result was that at 5'11", 155 lbs, I started varsity football, basketball, and baseball in my junior and senior years, made first team All-County and All-State in football and baseball, and was recruited by several colleges. Bad knees and poor finances kept me from competing in college, so I began coaching during my sophomore year.

My point here is that I wasn't bigger, faster, or stronger than anyone. I just worked harder, and more often. Don't let others put a ceiling on your potential. You have probably heard the phrase, "Your attitude determines your altitude." It's true. I got everything I could out of my skinny frame. Guys referred to me as "Bones." That only fueled my fire. The same can happen for you if you are willing to work hard at your sport. I hesitate to use the word "work" because if you are passionate about anything, the time you put into it never feels like work.

A great sportswriter, Jim Murray, once wrote, "When you think everything is hopeless, just remember Yogi Berra. That's because Yogi always exuded positivity, reflective of perhaps his most famous quote, "It ain't over til it's over." Yogi believed in himself when others doubted, mocked and even rejected him. He had to deal with people who made fun of his big ears. Some opponents even said, "Yogi, why don't you try to hit with your face?" Pretty low, huh? Yogi would just shrug his shoulders and rip a double. As an athlete, you can't let people rent space in your head for free. The best, and probably only, way to get a heckler to shut up is to perform your best. As Theodore Roosevelt once wrote, "The real hero is the man in the arena." I would add, "Not the idiot in the stands."

Yogi also believed that something good will happen when you give everything you have. He had an inner confidence, something every athlete needs. Here's an example of what you can learn from Yogi. When he was a 16 year old hopeful, he tried out for his hometown team, the St. Louis Cardinals, along with his friend and neighbor, Joe Garagiola. After the tryout, Yogi was told by Branch Rickey, the talent evaluator for the Cardinals, that he was too awkward and would never be a major league player. To make matters worse, Rickey signed Garagiola to a Cardinal farm contract and a $500 bonus.

Of course, Yogi was disappointed, but he believed he was better than Garagiola. He knew if he kept working hard and improving he would get a break. Which is exactly what happened. The man who ran the American Legion team Yogi played on happened to be a friend of George Weiss, then farm director for the New York Yankees. He called Weiss and said there was a pretty good, albeit unpolished, catcher in St. Louis, and it might be good to sign him. Weiss sent the Yankees' bullpen catcher, John Schulte, a St. Louis native, to the Berras' house and offered $500 to sign, plus $90 a month to play with Norfolk, the Yankees' Class B farm team. His hard work caught someone's eye, and thus began the career of one of America's most legendary athletes.

Think about it. In contrast to today's era of highly advanced scouting and recruiting, Yogi Berra was signed simply by word of mouth. To borrow a phrase from Rickey, the man who originally spurned Yogi, "Luck is the residue of design." All because Yogi continued to work hard and never gave up on himself, even when others did. His mindset is as relevant today as it was in the 1940's.

A Growth Mindset

Do you believe that you are already as good as you will ever be? Have you reached your full potential? If so, Carol Dweck, a Stanford psychologist, would say you have a fixed mindset. You don't feel that you need to improve, and you're not open to taking risks for fear of failure because failure would destroy the image you have of yourself. Holding on to a fixed mindset will stunt your growth. Think for a moment about a fruit. If it is green, it can grow. If it is ripe, it can only rot. The same is true for you as an athlete. Look at your athletic development in terms of a process rather than a result.

I laugh when people refer to an athlete as having reached his/her peak. How does anyone know when someone else is "in their prime"? Often, an arbitrary age is assigned to when an athlete has 'maxed out' and is starting to decline. Tell that to Mariano Rivera, who had one of his best years in his Hall of Fame career in his final season at age 40.

Hopefully, you have, or will develop, a growth mindset. A person with this mindset looks at failure as feedback, as a helpful hint of what not to do next time. Thomas Edison tried 113 different methods before he successfully invented the light bulb. He didn't look at those attempts as failures; he referred to them as "113 ways not to invent the light bulb." All successful people have encountered setbacks. Walt Disney went bankrupt five times. Abraham Lincoln lost many more elections than he won. These men, and many others, possessed a growth mindset. They took risks; they saw the bigger picture. You can do the same thing. I suggest you read *Mindset* by Carol Dweck. Her explanation of this concept is far more extensive than mine. I only wish I could have read her book when I was your age.

Deliberate Practice

"Practice makes perfect," or so I was told. Only, that's not correct. "Perfect practice makes perfect." Sounds silly, but it's true. Simply doing something over and over doesn't mean the end result is positive. Practice only makes permanent. What is really needed is deliberate practice. Hack golfers will go to a driving range and hit a bucket of balls before playing a round and call it "practice." That certainly isn't practice; it's barely exercise. Professional golfers take a bucket of balls and work with a club they don't have full command of yet. After determining what distance best suits their use of the club, they'll try to repeat the same swing over and over while trying to leave the ball within putting distance of the cup.

They might use a videotape to review their swing, and they always focus on a percentage, say 85% within ten feet. *That* is practicing with a purpose.

You can change your practice habits immediately. First, decide which skill you want to improve (e.g., dribbling with your off-hand or weaker foot, your flip turn in the pool or your first serve). Create drills that focus on your weakness using cones, a stopwatch or a drawn circle. Get comfortable with one motion and repeat it over and over and over. You don't want to simply shoot 50 jump shots. Instead, you want to shoot one jump shot correctly 50 times. As with the example of the pro golfer above, you will want to affix some type of measurement (a percentage, a time, etc.) and continually work to improve.

It might not seem like fun to practice deliberately, but you will enjoy seeing the results. Dieting isn't fun, until you step on the scale.

Play Against the Game, Not the Opponent

There are only a few things in life that you can actually control. Two of them are your effort and your preparation. That's why it is more beneficial for athletes to focus on the process rather than the outcome. As an athlete, you have no control over the weather conditions, the playing surface, the officials, and most often, your opponent. It only makes sense then that you concentrate on putting forth your best effort into mastering fundamentals and game situations every day in practice.

Two of the greatest coaches in sports' history, Vince Lombardi and John Wooden, understood the value of 100% effort every day in practice. Lombardi said, "The will to win isn't as important as the will to prepare." He believed that pro football games were won Monday through Saturday, not on Sunday. When Coach Wooden was asked which team he thought would win the NCAA Basketball Championship on

Monday night he replied, "The team that plays closest to how they practice." These two coaches aren't regarded as the best at their craft for no reason. You would be smart to accept their wisdom.

The easiest way I know to conquer game day jitters is to practice every day like it's a game. Then when the game arrives, you have already been there, done that. Far too many athletes take days off (mentally) during the week and try to gear it up on game day. That almost never works. They also get "psyched" for games against rival opponents. Again, that rarely works. They end up putting so much focus on the outcome, they forget the process – what they did daily to get ready. I have found that "psyched up" usually results in "psyched out" as soon as something goes wrong. The only way to feel confident is to know you have put your energy into preparing. Then you know you're ready.

P = P - I

Your Performance is equal to your Potential, minus the Interference. There is enough pressure on any athlete to perform at his/her best on game day without any external pressure (Interference). Coaches telling players: "This is a MUST win!" (Aren't all games important?) Fans reminding players: "We never lose to that team!" (Don't both squads have different players this year?) Teammates shouting: "Nobody beats us at our house!" (Won't your opponents say the same thing when you play on the road?) These are silly, pointless expressions that only serve to create more pressure and cause athletes to lose their focus.

Listen to any athlete being interviewed after a loss. Invariably you'll hear him/her say, "I just wasn't focused today." What he/she really means is "I wasn't able to play my best today because of outside distraction." You can't perform at your best when you are concerned with who is in the stands (your parents, boyfriend/girlfriend, recruiters). Thoughts like "It's now or never; it's do or die; it's up to me" can only serve to make you nervous.

The best way to minimize external noise is to keep things in perspective. The only MUST win in this country's history was World War II, and we won that on the road, long before you were born. Remind yourself that you are only playing a game, with your friends. Win or lose it's not the end of the world. It's already tomorrow in Australia!

Leadership - "It's About Others"

If you are selected to be a captain, you should feel honored that your coach respects your leadership potential. I use the word "potential" because being selected doesn't guarantee that you will be regarded as an effective leader. Upon your selection you will immediately have what is referred to as "ascribed status," meaning someone has given you a title/position. That's quite different from "achieved status," which is something you will need to earn from your teammates.

Being captain is a challenge and not a role for everyone. It certainly wasn't for me, despite being appointed to that position as a senior for my high school football team. As a 16 year old, I had no idea what my responsibilities were, and I was too caught up in notoriety to even consider the job description. Being introduced first over the PA on game days and regularly being out in front leading exercises boosted my ego significantly. I never stopped to realize that the most important quality a good captain possesses is an understanding that "It's about others." If you can't be selfless, meaning your individual statistics are more important to you than overall team success, you shouldn't be a captain.

In addition to demonstrating a team-first attitude, as a captain, you need to treat everyone with equal respect, from the potential all-state athlete to the manager. Your job is to make everyone feel included on and off the field. One way to do that is to shake hands or hi-five everyone before and/or after practice. You can also ask non-starters to lead the exercises and share responsibility for carrying equipment rather than assigning that role to underclassmen.

As a captain you need to be the first one to arrive and the last one to leave every day. Your coach is counting on you to make sure that there is no hazing or bullying on your team. This is a very serious issue. Roughly one-third of all teams experience some form of bullying or hazing. In some instances, coaches have been fired. If you do a good job of inclusion, you shouldn't have a problem. If you sense that there might be a problem, you need to speak directly to the players involved. They need to be told that picking on anyone on the team is unacceptable. You can't be paralyzed by WWOPT; your coach is counting on you. If your coach can't count on you, don't accept the position as captain; it's that simple.

You might be thinking, "I'm not a captain, how does this apply to me?" I can think of three solid reasons. First, just because you aren't a captain now doesn't mean that you won't be in the future. It's a great opportunity. Second, it's important that you understand the scope of the captain's responsibility in order to support him/her. Third, and probably most relevant, you might have a C.I.N.O. (Captain in Name Only). This will create a leadership vacuum. You might have the skill set and commitment to lead your teammates in the absence of an effective captain. As long as you continually put the team first, demonstrate passion, and reach out to everyone individually to ensure that they feel equally part of the team, you won't need an "ascribed title."

During Yogi's 18 year playing career there was no official Yankee captain. However, as a team-first player, Yogi was one of a few "unofficial" captains. He was always quick to reach out to his teammates. There are numerous such examples in Harvey Araton's wonderful book, *Driving Mr. Yogi*, which chronicles Yogi's relationship with Ron Guidry and their days at spring training in Tampa. Araton reveals how Yogi was always looking out for younger guys. Yogi took a shy Bobby Richardson, who hailed from South Carolina, and was intimidated by New York under his wing. He also protected a young pitching prospect named Tom Gorman in the 1952 World Series from a media onslaught when he took full responsibility for a crossed signal, allowing the Dodgers to win. Gorman later expressed his gratitude to Yogi for his unselfishness.

Perhaps the best example of Yogi's understanding of the importance of camaraderie among everyone on the team was his open welcome of Elston Howard, the team's first black player. Yogi spent most of his time on the road with Elston, going to movies, going out to eat, even going clothes shopping. Their relationship was crucial to the franchise since Yankee management was late to integration – they were the 13th of 16 teams to bring in a black player. When the Yankees wanted to get Elston's bat in the lineup in the late 1950's, Yogi agreed to move to the outfield so Elston could be the regular catcher.

Arlene Howard, Elston's wife, bought the very first brick in the plaza outside the YBM. She told Dave Kaplan, director of the museum, that it was Yogi who made Elston "truly feel part of the Yankee family." Everyone who loves baseball knows what a great player Yogi was. Our mission at the Yogi Berra Museum is to let our visitors know what a great leader and teammate he was.

The most highly publicized athlete of your time is probably Michael Jordan. Some consider him the best basketball player ever. He's appeared in numerous commercials, one which features kids saying, "I want to be like Mike!" While there's little argument that he was one of the best athletes of his generation, and he was at his best when the spotlight was at his brightest, when some light was shed on his personal life the light dimmed. I mean no disrespect to Jordan. I think he was terrific, but I think it would be more appropriate for kids to want to "play like Mike." With Yogi, who also appeared in numerous commercials, the light shines just as bright on his personal life as it does on his Hall of Fame career. My intention is to encourage you to think, "I want to be like Yogi."

Athletes

Everyone on the team has an equal opportunity to be thought of as the best player FOR the team. The shared goal then should be to do the team-first things that will make you the best teammate. Remember, "It's about others."

As a teammate, Yogi took great pride in the family feeling of his Yankee teams. There wasn't anything a teammate wouldn't do for another. Although the Yankees in 1955 became one of the last teams to integrate, Yogi and his teammates warmly embraced Elston Howard. Yogi and Elston, both catchers, ate together on the road. Other players such as Hank Bauer, Mickey Mantle and Phil Rizzuto (whom Howard fondly called "my great white father") were also supportive allies and helped ease Howard's assimilation during a time of racial tensions in baseball and throughout the country.

The movie *42* - the story of Jackie Robinson breaking baseball's longstanding color barrier - accurately depicts the moral climate of the country. There was overt racism, even among several of Robinson's own teammates.

In fact, Larry Doby, who became the second African-American player in baseball, joining the Cleveland Indians only 11 weeks after Robinson's debut, not only had to endure racist taunts from other teams, but was initially ostracized by almost his entire team. Doby, who later became a neighbor of Yogi's in Montclair, never forgot how certain people stepped up and showed him acceptance. Foremost was Yogi, who according to Doby, always engaged in friendly chatter with him, seeing how he was doing, encouraging him to hang in there.

Being inclusive is what sports should be all about. As Yogi once said in his own inimitable style, "If you can play, then you can play." Meaning, one should be judged by his/her talent, not race, religion, ethnicity or sexual orientation. If you can play, then you can play.

While racial equality was a great divide in America before and during the Civil Rights movement, surely LGBT equality is currently one of our country's most polarizing issues. Despite our supposed enlightened culture, many high school, college and professional athletes struggle with the notion of having a gay teammate.

To that point, Yogi became one of the nation's most prominent athletic figures to support the work of Athlete Ally, a nonprofit organization designed to eradicate homophobia in sports. His Museum partnered with Athlete Ally and installed an exhibit called "Allyship," highlighting examples of teammates who challenged prejudices against a minority group. For example, the great Ted Williams used his Hall of Fame speech in the mid-1960's to advocate for the inclusion of Negro Leaguers into the Hall. It was a bold stance and caused quite a stir at the time, but not surprising from a man who was an outspoken supporter of minorities in baseball, and went out of his way to welcome the Red Sox' first black player, Pumpsie Green.

Some of the greatest athletes ever were some of the greatest team players. Yankee legend Mickey Mantle, who played alongside Yogi for 13 seasons, despite debilitating pain and injuries was always there for his teammates. Mantle himself said he wanted to be remembered for that aspect of his career more than any of his prodigious accomplishments. Indeed, his plaque in Monument Park in Yankee Stadium is headlined: "Mickey Mantle: A Great Teammate."

The example set forth by Yogi and Mickey Mantle and their Yankee teammates' lives today with the Yogi Berra Museum & Learning Center's creation of the Best Teammate Award, a recognition of the most selfless student-athletes in the Super Essex Conference in Essex County, New Jersey. Each year, 37 student-athletes, nominated by their coaches and athletic directors, are feted not for their scoring exploits or other personal achievements. They are celebrated for their team-first attitude. They have obviously learned that it's about others. It all begins with a choice. It all begins with your choice.

Athletes' Pillow Test

Before you go to sleep each night, ask yourself, "Did I do everything I could today to improve as a student, athlete, and person? Or Do I wish I had?"

8 Takeaways for Athletes from Yogi:

1. Play as many sports as you can in order to stay in shape year round. Yogi did.

2. Give 100% of your energy to whatever sport you play. Anything worth doing is worth doing well.

3. Listen to your coaches and other players.
   Bill Dickey taught Yogi to become a better catcher.
   Yogi, in turn, helped Elston Howard.

4. Remember that talent is overrated. Only you can determine your athletic ceiling. Yogi was 5'8", 180 lbs, not a Hall of Fame body by any stretch.

5. Being on time is important. One of Yogi's cardinal rules. He was always early.

6. Keep the game simple. When asked what he thought about when he was hitting, Yogi said, "hitting." "See the ball, hit the ball" was his motto.

7. Try to minimize external interference (noise).
   Yogi believed that a "full mind caused an empty bat."

8. Aspire to be the best teammate. That's the best way to gain everyone's respect. It wasn't only Yogi's stats that made him an American icon.

8 Suggested Readings:

1. *The Talent Code* – Daniel Coyle
2. *Mindset* – Carol Dweck
3. *The Inner Game of Tennis* – W. Timothy Gallway
4. *Play Like A Champion* – Dick DeVenzio
5. *Toughness* – Jay Bilas
6. *Think Better, Win More!* – Rob Gilbert, Mike Tully
7. *A Sense of Where You Are* – John McPhee
8. *You Can Observe A Lot By Watching: What I Learned About Teamwork From the Yankees and Life* – Yogi Berra

8 Suggested Videos: (YouTube)

1. *Jayson McElwain*
2. *Kyle Maynard*
3. *Ben Comen*
4. *Facing the Giants* (Death Crawl scene)
5. *Ray Lewis at Elon College*
6. *Evan Ruggiero – One-legged Tap Dancer*
7. *Vision Quest*
8. *Minnesota Runner Falls Down, Still Wins*

Note to Athletes:

Don't stop reading now that you have information that will help you reach your full potential as an athlete. Keep reading the next two parts to discover what coaches and parents will be asked to do to help you. To improve the culture of sports, we need to establish common ground among you, your coaches, and your parents. Do your part to the best of your ability. Take the "pillow test" every night. Before you go to sleep, ask yourself, "Did I do everything I could today to improve as a student, athlete, and person?" or "Do I wish I had?"

Before you were probably born, there was a commonly held belief that sports build character. That myth has been totally dispelled. It's currently more commonly recognized that sports reveal character. Regrettably, we've reached a point where most newspapers devote space on a daily basis to chronicling instances where athletes run afoul of the law. DUI, domestic abuse, gun possession and even murder have been reported with regularity. Some would argue that the failings of athletes are reflective of a trend in society in general. Perhaps that's true. That doesn't mean that you need to be a part of that trend. As an athlete, at times you will be held to a higher standard. Don't regard that as a burden because you can positively shape the way you are regarded by the decisions you make and the actions you take. The majority of athletes appreciate the opportunity they have to compete and do so knowing that competing with character matters. Make up your mind that you want to be part of the majority.

With the announcement of his intended retirement, Derek Jeter's legacy as a Yankee became a hot topic. Would he be thought of in the same light as the Mt. Rushmore of all-time Yankee greats: Ruth, Gehrig, DiMaggio and Mantle? While that question is certain to produce a lively debate, I'd like to propose a revised Mt. Rushmore of Yankee greats that would definitely include the Yankee captain. My group would consist of hard-working, team-first players, who not only produced Hall of Fame numbers on the diamond, but men who never tarnished the Yankee name in any way, and were admired as much for their character as their statistics. My group would include: Lou Gehrig, Yogi Berra, Derek Jeter, and Mariano Rivera. You might not be able to match the talent of these Yankee greats, but you certainly can mimic their character.

There's no better feeling than connecting with student/athletes. The goal of our Captains Seminar is to provide them with specific strategies to help them lead their teams.

Outlining the programs offered at the Yogi Berra museum for athletic directors from the Super Essex Conference.

Former Giants QB, Scott Brunner, and President and CEO of Investors Bank, Kevin Cummings, present a Best Teammate Award to Yaramo Dione. Investors is the sponsor of the dinner/awards ceremony and of a number of programs at the Museum.

Occasionally schools from a conference pair up and send captains and coaches to the Museum. In this instance, Livingston HS and West Orange HS partner for an afternoon session on Sportsmanship.

Gian Paul Gonzalez tells his "All In" story at a fall Sports Symposium at Millburn HS to all fall athletes. A dynamic speaker, Gian Paul has represented the Museum at numerous venues.

Dr. Gilbert demonstrates his A.C.E. (action creates energy) theory with an exercise for captains at the Museum. A highly noted motivational speaker, he has given over 5,000 talks to a wide range of audiences.

Working with student/athletes always produces a smile, especially when they're volleyball players who just happen to be your nieces, Lindsay and Maggie.

Part 2 - Coaches

"No written word, nor spoken plea
Can teach our youth what they should be.
Not all the books on all the shelves,
It's what the teachers are themselves."

-Anonymous

The most important question for a coach: Do you want to be successful or significant?

It might not always occur to us as coaches when we're at practice or at a game, but those two hours might be the best part of our athletes' day. More often than not, we know little about their home life. That's not to suggest that most athletes come from troubled or dysfunctional families. However, some do. Even youngsters who come from a stable domestic situation are looking for additional adult voices. For many, that voice belongs to a coach. Having an influence on a student/athlete is the reason why most coaches become involved in the profession. Others do it because it gives them an identity, or because it's a pathway to notoriety and financial gain. What's your reason? How will you measure your level of success?

On a professional level, coaches are judged by how many games and/or championships they win. That's one barometer. What about on an amateur level? Will you regard your final tally of wins versus losses as a measurement of your coaching ability? The problem with that perspective is the reality that when you die, your "success" dies with you. A significant coach, on the other hand, is one whose success lives on because he/she has helped others become successful. A significant coach is one who has developed personal relationships with his/her players which last well beyond the expiration of eligibility.

To be clear, a coach can be both successful and significant; it depends on the coach's vision of his/her players. Are they regarded as a means to an end as he/she tries to climb the coaching ladder, constantly searching for a bigger job on a higher level? Or does the coach recognize that his/her sole task is the athletic development and personal growth of every individual on the team? Does the coach want a great team or a great program? Does the coach emphasize the outcome over the process? What drives you?

Perhaps the best way to express my point is to relate a post-season interview I once read. After his team completed its schedule, a reporter asked a coach, "How would you assess your team's season?" He replied, "Ask me in 20 years." I took this to mean his job was to prepare his young men to be quality individuals in whatever career path they followed. Their character development was more significant to him than their won-loss record. In all honesty, while I knew I had a chance to impact young lives when I first started coaching, I was fixated on winning. I wasn't thinking about upward mobility, but I believed that my reputation as a coach was inexorably linked to my record. I think most novice coaches think the way I did at first. Fortunately, I was mentored by men who "got it." I had to learn that it wasn't about me – it was about others, specifically the players. It was their team, their years, not mine. Like Yogi always says, "We had our shot. Now it's their turn."

What I eventually learned was that a coach, even a "great" one like I thought I was, can't control everything. I remember asking a friend of mine to come to a game when I was coaching a 9th grade basketball team. We won convincingly; I couldn't wait to hear his affirmation of my coaching prowess. Instead he said, "You're not a coach. You're an air traffic controller.

You yell at all five guys on offense and defense. You look like a marionette trying to pull the strings of five puppets at one time!" I was stung. How could he not recognize that my team won because of my coaching? Once I shook off the hurt, and it took awhile, I realized that my friend had given me the best advice I would ever receive: Players win games, not coaches. The longer you stay in the profession, the more you realize how true that statement is. The sooner you, as a coach, learn it, the sooner you'll focus more on your players' growth than your ego. I had to learn it the hard way.

I also learned that there are "paychecks" that you can get from coaching that you can't get in any other profession when you put your athletes' success above your own. Players aren't a means to an end; they are the end. The number and quality of relationships you develop with your players will tell you all you need to know about success and significance. Your hourly wage may be minimal, but you have the power to create a lifetime of dividends.

All coaches need mentoring. I had two great mentors at Montclair State, Ollie Gelston and Mike Cohen.

Pop's Story

Russ Monica was an offensive lineman at Fordham University. He played on the same line as Vince Lombardi, when they were referred to as "The Seven Blocks of Granite." There were no face masks worn in those days, and "Pop," as I later came to know him as my high school football coach, wore the scars of four years of college and several more in a semi-pro league as a badge of honor. Most notably, when he faced midfield, his nose pointed to the end zone. He wasn't tall as linemen go, barely reaching six feet, but he had broad shoulders and hands the size of a catcher's mitt.

I first met Russ when he came to a game in which I played as an eighth grader, and afterwards asked me if I planned on attending Our Lady of the Valley H.S. in Orange, NJ. Since I lived in that parish and had attended grade school there, it was natural that I would go to the high school. The chance to play football for such a well-respected coach made it a no-brainer. From day one at the Valley, I felt a closeness to Pop. He was a history teacher at Orange H.S., where my father worked as a custodian. I can't tell you how special I felt on September 1, 1963, the first day of practice, when Coach Monica referred to me by name. "Today is the beginning of a career as one of the best receivers we'll ever have at the Valley. Say hello to Jack McCarthy!" he announced in the locker room. My birth name is John, my dad was known as Jack, but coach could have called me Dumbo, and I still would have been on Cloud Nine!

It didn't take long for everyone on the team to recognize that Pop was a different kind of coach. Despite his large frame, he was a gentle man, a gentleman. He greeted everyone with a warm, broad smile and a handshake that simultaneously included a tap on the back of the shoulder. During practice, alumni would regularly stop by to visit him. His face lit up.

He'd excuse himself, turn drills over to an assistant coach, and walk over to the distant bleachers and sit for at least half an hour. He didn't speak much. Mostly, he asked questions, grinned and nodded. He'd come back, take his hat off, rub his mostly bald head, put the cap back on, rub his chin and smile. He looked like someone who had just visited a long lost relative. Then he'd bark, "Let's get to work!" At those moments I had one thought: "I want to be just like him some day."

We had no athletic trainer, so pre-game ankle taping fell to Pop. Anyone, including guys who wouldn't get in the game if lightning hit and only 10 players were left standing, who needed to be taped, got the same, first-rate treatment. Pop would finish the taping, pat both sides of the ankle gently and say, "Have a big game, Fella." He would then enter the larger area of the locker room and begin to deliver what we would later come to call "the needle". His pre-game talks, fashioned after legendary football coach at Notre Dame, Knute Rockne, were spellbinding. Players sat facing each other on wooden benches, hanging on every word, every intonation. He began with a slow pace and a slow rate. He'd walk faster, then speak quicker. We could feel the blood rushing in our veins. He talked about playing hard for each other; how we had a sense of camaraderie; how we loved one another, and loved playing for the Valley. He'd build to a crescendo with "This team can't wait to get at you, but that's alright. That's alright because we can't wait to get at them, because we're gonna block, block, block, and tackle, tackle, tackle like we've never done before! Because we are Valley! Now go out there and get 'em!" We nearly fell over each other, and the benches, trying to get out of the door.

What we loved about Pop, and still do, is who he was as a man. He wasn't afraid to show his passion. We were 16, he was 60, and yet he always let his emotions pour out in front of us. He had played semi-pro ball, and he was still able to make us feel that our high school game mattered, that we mattered.

There's a saying that, "People might forget what you say to them, but they'll never forget how you make them feel." Those of us who played for Coach Pop Monica will always remember both. He was successful and significant. He is the reason many of us went into coaching. We wanted our players to feel the same way about us that we feel about him. Since we could never pay him back, we tried to pay it forward with our players.

You may not have had a Pop Monica in your past, but you must have someone you feel indebted to for helping you in some way. As a coach, you have an opportunity to thank that person by treating your charges the way you were treated. When Don Mattingly changed his uniform number as manager of the Dodgers to number 8, he did so as a tribute to Yogi, and stated that he will wear that number until he retires. To me, that gesture certainly proves Yogi's significance as Mattingly's coach during his Yankee days.

Coaches

Is your goal to be successful or significant? When players graduate, how will they remember you? What do you do on a daily basis that will influence their recollection?

The Coach's Dozen

Coaching has become harder every year. The pull of travel and elite teams has in some instances reduced the role of the traditional coach. Parental interference has also drained some of the energy of even veteran coaches. While these developments can't always be controlled, they can be managed. Coaches need to be pro-active. Here are a dozen things you can do to create a healthy, competitive athletic environment, on the way to a significant career.

1. Be a professional at all times.

- Remember you are a teacher 24/7.
- Keep your composure at all times.
- Praise in public; criticize in private.
- Stay away from social media.

Once you accept a job in the public domain, you sacrifice some level of privacy. Social media instantly provides access to whatever coaches do or say. In fact, some coaches have been secretly taped in locker rooms; several coaches have lost their job for comments during an emotional rant. The best way to protect yourself as a coach is to stay away from Facebook, Twitter, etc., and more importantly, to remember that as a coach, you are a teacher 24/7. If you act professionally at all times, you won't jeopardize your position. The field or gym should be regarded as your classroom. You wouldn't curse or berate a student in your math or Spanish class, so don't do either to an athlete on your team. It's also helpful to remember to praise in public and criticize in private. In general, individuals don't respond well to being 'called out' in front of their peers. Also, try to coach every athlete the way you would want your son or daughter to be coached.

2. Don't try to do everything yourself.

- Hire quality assistants who complement you.
- Refer to assistants as "associates."
- Appoint captains whom you can trust.
- Give players a voice.

In any group venture, a workforce, or a team, individuals grow tired of hearing one voice over and over. They also benefit from more than one point of view. It is vital that a coach hire staff who will complement (with an "e," not an "i") him/her. If you are generally laid back, you need to surround yourself with energetic, vocal associates. If you are bundle of energy and a rapid-fire talker, you need to hire an associate who will provide a calming influence. A "yes man/woman" may boost your ego, but he/she won't help you when you need an alternate plan. It is also important to select captains who you feel reflect your values and buy into your approach. Letting kids vote for captains, in my opinion, is a mistake. You can't be everywhere and supervise everyone on the field, in the locker room or in the hallways. You need captains who will assure you that there will be absolutely no hazing on their watch. It only takes one incident of bullying or abuse for you to get fired. Tell your captains what you expect from them and provide opportunities for them to speak before and after practices and/or games.

3. Provide an out of season regimen.

- Encourage participation in a second sport.
- Emphasize the importance of maintaining good grades.
- Require some type of community service.
- Explore team-building opportunities.

One of the biggest problems among coaches is 'poaching' or forcing specialization. Don't contribute to the problem. Athletes benefit most by learning to compete. The more sports they play, the more opportunities they have to test themselves. Forcing one of your players to focus solely on your sport will engender criticism from other coaches in your school, and possibly from parents. You might also be placing an athlete in a difficult position, which may lead to resentment. Instead, help your athletes recognize that they are part of a larger community, as a student of the school, and a citizen in the town. Remind them that their behavior should never bring negative attention to either. Monitor their academic performance. Your job isn't over at the end of the season. The goal of every coach should be to help every athlete create a healthy lifestyle, rooted in year-round fitness, and to obtain a college degree. Coaches who focus solely on keeping athletes eligible for their season do their players a tremendous disservice.

4. Remain positive.

- Focus on the next play, not the last one.
- Stress bounce-back ability (no hanging heads)
- Make it a point to publicly praise people (players, managers, etc.)
- Criticize the performance, not the player.

Over the course of the season, there will be numerous setbacks ranging from injuries to tough losses. How your team responds to these challenges will be determined, in large measure, by how you, as the coach, respond. If your focus is on getting better, every 'next play' and/or new day offers an opportunity for growth. Dwelling on the past, "calling players out," or sulking will only lower morale. It requires mental toughness to maintain a positive outlook. Keep in mind that a setback is an opportunity for a comeback.

As a coach you need to seize this 'teachable moment' by encouraging players to hang in there and work harder to limit further disappointment. This is probably the most important life lesson you can teach your athletes. As I said to athletes in Part I, Hall of Fame high school basketball coach, Bob Hurley, once said, "How we handle failure defines our character."

One of Yogi's strengths as a manager was his ability to remain positive no matter how bleak the circumstances. Midway through the 1973 season when he was managing the Mets they were mired in last place. When pressed by reporters to comment on the Mets' cellar-dwelling position, Yogi responded with his inimitable line, "It ain't over 'til it's over." The Mets went on to win the National League pennant. As I said earlier, when you find yourself in a tough spot as a coach, remember: Do What Yogi Would Do!

5. Stress fundamentals.

- Confidence comes from mastering skills, not from coaches' words.

- Mastery of skills comes through conscientious repetition.

- Practice requires intensity.

- Proper sleep and nutrition need constant reinforcement.

Study after study confirms that most adolescents lack sleep and a balanced diet. Throw in rigorous physical demands and a packed scheduled and it is apparent that something has to give. Usually it's performance. For far too long, coaches have given lip service to recognition of the demands on student/athletes. You can change that. Find a nutritionist to speak to your team before each season. Monitor pre-game meals and provide healthy snacks in the locker room. Also, don't be afraid to institute bed checks the night before a game. Doing these things tells players that you care about their well-being. A healthier athlete can bring more intensity to practice and games, allowing him/her to better focus during repetitive drills. Once an athlete feels confident, earned through 'sweat equity,' you won't need to deliver 'pep talks.'

6. Employ a growth mindset.

- No one has reached full potential.
- Emphasize the word "yet." "I can't do it <u>yet</u>."
- Let players know <u>why</u> they need deliberate practice.
- Place focus on getting better, not winning.

The phrase, "A man's reach should extend beyond his grasp," is good to remember here. As a coach, you are always looking for improvement in your team. Even after a victory, there will be something that can be done better. Perfection may not be attainable, but excellence is. That's what all teams should strive to attain. Along the way, players need to be told, "We need to get better at _____." When they become discouraged, you can say, "We can't do _____ yet, but we'll get there." If you focus on the outcome (winning), and not the process, you'll fall into a fixed-mindset ("We're not very good."). Good coaches are always forward-looking, always searching for ways to improve. Remember, the journey is the destination.

7. Teach players to 'play against the game,' not the opponent or officials.

- The focus should be on only things that can be controlled.
- Most games are <u>lost</u> (errors, walks, turnovers) rather than won.
- Remain calm – players take their cue from their coach.
- Stay off game officials (That's a built in excuse).

Unlike a school musical or Broadway play, sports are fluid. There's no provision for blocking a scene, and there are variables outside of the performer's control. The key for a coach is a myopic focus on things he/she can control, namely preparation and comportment. Coaches win practice; players win games when they execute what they practice. There are constants in most sports. For instance, an opponent can't impact a free throw, a first serve, a fly ball, water in a pool, the distance to a bowling pin, etc. Therefore, as a coach, you need to design practices around the fundamental skills (blocking, tackling, shooting, serving) which can be employed in a competitive contest in order to influence the outcome. John Wooden believed that the team that plays closest to how it practices has the best chance of being successful. It's worth noting that Wooden, who won more NCAA basketball championships than anyone, never said the word "win". Focus on the process and live with the results.

Measuring Real Success

The ultimate goal of every coach should be to try to put every student-athlete on a path to earn a college diploma. Any attempt to manipulate the system in order to keep a player eligible is short-sighted, selfish, and unprofessional.

8. Hold players accountable.

- Apply school rules consistently to everyone.
- Being late should not be tolerated.
- Make no disqualifications your seasonal goal.
- Don't allow players to question officials or trash talk opponents.

One of the most important personal traits a coach must demonstrate is consistency. School personnel, as well as athletes, need to know exactly what to expect from a coach. Will he/she consistently enforce rules, or play favorites? Will he/she expect behaviors from athletes that he/she won't personally demonstrate? Once players sense that you have a different set of rules for four-star players or yourself, your credibility is lost. You need a clear vision on accountability, which you must preach, teach and live by. You can't show up late and demand punctuality. You can't preach "playing against the game," and then get thrown out of a game for arguing with officials. Once you make clear how you expect your players to comport themselves, you must serve as their role model. You need to convey the importance of treating opponents, officials, rules and facilities with respect. Any deviation must be addressed promptly. It's better to lose a game by sitting a star player than to lose your team by not sitting him/her.

9. Coach every athlete, not just the stars.

- Reward things other than performance.
- Find playing time for as many players as possible.
- Teach players how to compete.
- Rotate responsibility for carrying equipment.

Adolescents are more perceptive than adults realize. Coaches spend hours during the off-season and in pre-season talking about team unity and the need for everyone to buy into a team-first philosophy. Then after the season at the team's award function, they spend most of their time lauding the team's MVP. What happened to personal sacrifice, effort and all for one? Don't fall into this trap (tradition?) of rewarding only the best performer. Instead, reward what you preached: most hustle, best teammate, etc. During the season, allow players to earn playing time by performing well in competitive drills and scrimmages.

Some coaches fear that continual open competition will destabilize a starting rotation and negatively impact team chemistry. Many others believe it will create more spirited practices which push starters to maximize their ability and prepare substitutes for action when called upon. The longer you coach, the more you'll come to realize that giving more individuals playing time will make your job easier and more enjoyable.

10. Be careful when you select your team.

- Document tryout performance.

- Avoid using a cut list.

- Find capable managers.

- Keep a 'cheerleader.'

These days tryouts have become less 'open' than in the past. Some natural selection has occurred as a result of summer leagues, camps and off-season weight training. Still, as a coach, you need to be open-minded about newcomers to your team. A number of coaches who have had a high turnout for a much smaller roster have taken to maintaining data for competitive drills in order to explain their selections when challenged by parents. This situation is usually present with teams that have experienced significant success in the past and enjoy a tradition of championship level play. Regardless of the number of roster deletions you need to make, don't use a cut list. Instead, meet with individuals, thank them for their interest and effort, and explain why they aren't presently capable of making your team. A cut list embarrasses an adolescent and will probably result in a phone call to your AD or principal. Besides, it's impersonal and not the best way to treat young people. Treat those who try out for your team the way you would want a coach to treat your child.

11. Avoid "lose – lose" situations.

- Avoid surprises – parents hate them.
- Don't step on tradition.
- Limit your use of social media.
- Never be alone with a player (male or female).

Often, well-meaning coaches find themselves in a difficult position when they don't consider potential repercussions for their actions. They might arrive new to a school and try to change a losing culture while establishing a new brand, not realizing that traditions die hard, and those who have upheld them may be easily offended. In an effort to be totally accessible, they give their cell number to everyone, not realizing that many people don't respect others' privacy or don't respect boundaries. They might offer a player a ride home or a shoulder to cry on in a private area, not recognizing how this might be viewed/ misinterpreted by an outsider or a parent. It's unfortunate that coaches have to be so guarded about their interaction with players, but that's the reality we live with because a few coaches have violated the public trust. It's best to remain private, limit the number of people with access to your cell number, stay off Facebook and Twitter, and be sure someone is with you, or within viewing distance, when you have a private session with a student/athlete. "Better safe than sorry" has lasted as a cliché for a reason.

12. Manage parental contact.

- Conduct a preseason meeting.
- Provide a calendar of practices and games.
- Establish a 24 hour, e-mail only rule.
- Schedule a 'skills' practice and invite parents.

Once you select your team, invite parents to a Saturday practice. Provide refreshments. Let them see you at work, in your "classroom." Share your ideas on how you like to see the game played. Tell them what you expect from your players. Be sure this practice is entirely a "skills" practice with assistants and/or managers keeping statistics. This might provide parents with a more realistic view of how their son/daughter compares to other players in terms of mastery of fundamentals. Explain how you plan to help their youngster grow as a person and give them your e-mail address. Suggest a 24-hour delay before making a post-game contact. Tell them what you will respond to (family situations that may impact on attendance or performance), and what you will not respond to (questions on playing time or coaching techniques). Explain that you have informed players that they can come to talk to you about anything; that you believe players are old enough now to be responsible for themselves. If at any point parents feel the need to meet with you personally, they should set up an appointment with your AD and you'll make yourself available. Express your belief and hope that such a meeting will never be necessary.

Climate Control

Players and parents take their cue from coaches. If you rant and rave on the sidelines and constantly question game officials, so will your players and parents. Coaches need to model appropriate behavior at all times.

Whether you are coaching in high school (above) or college (right), the coach needs to calmly explain what he/she expects.

A 20th reunion with players is the best tribute a coach can receive. Coach Gelston and I with former MSC Indians from the mid 80's.

Things I Learned as a Coach

Over-coaching

An expressed goal of adults who work with young people is to get them to think for themselves. When I first started coaching, I was the ultimate hypocrite. 'Control freak' doesn't begin to describe my behavior. As I gained experience and observed long-tenured coaches, it began to sink in that my style was actually retarding the growth of my players. Luckily, I worked under established coaches who actually let their players play. They knew the secret: Coaches win in practice; players win games.

Consider a classroom teacher preparing his/her students for a state-mandated test or the SAT. Once the test arrives, students must perform their best with no teacher input. All of the preparation has to be done in class, in advance of the test. It should be the same way with sports. A coach has a preseason and daily practices to teach his/her athletes what they need to do to perform at their best on game day. As a coach, you need to thoroughly plan every day. Your challenge then is to get your players to play like they practice.

It's true that games are more fluid than a test, and there are more variables. I get that, but there's a difference between making adjustments during timeouts and half-time and micro-managing every possession. I watch individuals continually pace, question every call, and never cease barking commands. That's not coaching. If you want to be a play-by-play announcer, do it. Let a teacher take your place as the coach – someone who will let the kids play. Perhaps the following story will illustrate how I learned a hard lesson about over-coaching.

I was coaching a JV basketball team and we were playing on the road. The game was tied at 54 with 15 seconds to go when we got a steal. My point guard was on his way in to score the winning basket when a kid from the opposing team ran him down from behind and fouled him. In the process, the defender injured his leg. TIME OUT. While the trainer attended to the injured player, I called my team over to the bench to go over all of the possible scenarios. First, I told our shooter that I had every confidence in him that he would convert both free throws, but I wanted to cover all of the possibilities. "If Billy makes both free throws, we'll drop to half court and play man-to-man defense, no fouls. If he makes only one, we'll pick up in our 2-2-1 trap and take away all driving lanes. If we don't get either free throw, we'll play man-to-man full and trap when we can. If we don't get a steal in the first 10 seconds, foul either number 12 or number 33. We have one time-out left if you need it. Everyone got it?" They all nodded yes.

Billy stepped to the line. CLANG. I clapped my hands to encourage him. Again he toed the free throw line. CLANG. They rebounded the second miss and quickly raced up court. Their coach, who hadn't had time to huddle with his players during the time-out because he was tending to his injured player, rose up, made a circular motion with one hand as he shouted "ON-DE-LAY...ON-DE-LAY." Until that point I hadn't even noticed that he didn't speak English (though all of his players were Irish, Polish or Italian). My team had been "coached up" for every conceivable situation, or so I thought. Our opponent was armed only with "ON-DE-LAY." One quick outlet pass, another to the top of the key where a 5'3 lefty threw up a desperation jumper. Swish! We lose 56-54.

I shook hands with the coach and weakly said, "Good game coach." He nodded and smiled. Of course he nodded. He didn't speak English! After we showered, we walked dejectedly to our bus. I put my arm around Billy and told him I wouldn't have wanted anyone else at the foul line at that point in the game. He responded, "Thanks, Coach," paused, then added, "Maybe we should use that ON-DE-LAY play next game."

Relationships, not rules

If a coach has a hundred rules, then he/she has to police them, and kids being kids are going to break them. Coaching requires an individual to wear many hats: teacher, substitute parent, psychologist, nutritionist, guidance counselor, etc. Why add cop to your job description? Besides, rules without relationships often lead to rebellion.

Think back to when you were a kid. Remember when your parents were angry with you? If you were anything like me, their anger didn't really bother you. You knew they'd get over it. It was a completely different story when they were "disappointed" in you. The paralyzing feeling that overwhelmed you existed because a relationship was being threatened. As a coach, you hope to build relationships with your players that aren't based on fear of consequences, but rather a bond that shouldn't be broken. Hopefully you'll engender a mutual respect that makes a litany of rules unnecessary.

At Montclair State University I was fortunate to work under the dean of New Jersey coaches, Ollie Gelston. He had only one rule: Be at the right place, at the right time, and do the right thing. The inherent beauty of this rule is that it requires continual self-assessment on the part of an athlete. Right time? Easy. Right place? Easy. Right thing? Not so easy. Having athletes ask themselves, "Am I doing the right thing?" is vital for their personal growth and accountability. They have to decide without access to a rule book. If you're ever asked, especially by younger athletes, "Coach, how do I know if I'm doing the right thing?" Tell them to pretend their grandmother's standing next to them. They'll know what to do.

Relationships Not Rules

The more rules you have, the more you have to enforce. Put the responsibility on players to be at the right place, at the right time, and do the right thing. Rules without relationships are worthless.

Success Leaves Clues

My colleague at Montclair State, Dr. Rob Gilbert, tells his students that if they want to be successful at something, find someone to mentor you who is already doing what you want to do and doing it well. I wish someone had given me this advice when I first started coaching. I played multiple sports, with a good degree of success, so of course I thought I knew everything. It was simple – do exactly what my coaches did. How hard could it be? As a junior in college, I found out.

My initial coaching job was as a freshman basketball coach at my high school ($300 for the season). The following year I landed additional positions in JV soccer (a sport I never played) and JV baseball. Playing three sports for four years in high school in no way prepared me for coaching three sports. I had no idea what being responsible for others' performance and well-being entailed. I tried to mimic my former coaches. That didn't work, primarily because I was too wrapped up in my own experience at that time to watch what they were doing and how they were doing it. I survived my baptism under fire and was fortunate to work under some great coaches. I studied them carefully, constantly asked why they did something, and experimented with my teams to find my own coaching voice. I "borrowed" ideas from every clinician and read books by and about coaches I admired.

Presently I teach Coaching Principles/Problems at MSU. The first assignment I give my students is an observation of at least two coaches before, during, and after a game. They're also required to read a book about a coach or coaching in general. Additionally, I bring in five athletic directors and several coaches to share their philosophies and experiences with my future coaches. Dr. Gilbert is spot on when he says "success leaves clues."

Inspirational Videos

If "A picture is worth a thousand words," why do we as coaches talk so much when trying to motivate players? My excuse as a late Baby Boomer is that I grew up when print media was at its apex, and there was no paucity of great speakers (JFK, MLK, Fulton Sheen, etc.) Throw in 12 years of Catholic school education where I was continually told to sit quietly and listen, and it's no wonder I am generally an auditory learner.

It wasn't until I became a teacher that I became aware of other modalities. Put a pile of wood in front of some people and they can build a tree house. Others will ask, "Where are the directions?" Still others will say, "Let me watch you build one, then I'll do it." No wonder so many of my peers got lost in the singular, didactic method the nuns followed.

When I started coaching, I talked far too much. My wife says I still do. I am who I am. Thanks to Dr. Gilbert I've come to learn the power of the video. His students are mesmerized by the images on the screen of people who overcome significant obstacles, including birth defects, on a path to greatness. At the end of the semester his students cite watching clips he shows as inspiring them to make changes in their lives. His iPad is a treasure trove filled with countless moving stories of personal achievement. Some of the videos he uses you'll find at the end of each chapter under the heading: 8 Suggested Videos. I suggest that you view the ones listed for athletes, as well as the ones I'll list for parents after Part 3. Let's face it, we live in a visual age. While I'm thankful that the nuns made me a better listener, I've learned the merits of YouTube. Unless you're a dinosaur like I was, you'll come to see that motivating your players with DVDs will work for YOU, TOO!

Coach Everyone, Not Just the Stars

Living in a celebrity-driven culture, it's difficult not to be hypnotized by star power. ESPN, my lifeline, doesn't help. Every night they present us with superhuman feats by megastars. We see the reverse dunk, the 450 foot homerun, the scissor kick goal and the chip in from a deep bunker. We never see the bounce pass that creates a lay-in, the sacrifice bunt, the clearing kick or the recovery shot from the rough. The result is that our attention is drawn away from the little details that win games and championships and from the players whose effort and unselfishness help stars shine.

I still remember a time when I was guilty of focusing on my star player, Luke, instead of helping everyone on the team develop. We ran all of our offense through him. It made sense at the time since he was far and away our best offensive threat. His teammates nicknamed him, "Water," because he could drain it from anywhere. The day before the state tournament, he jammed the thumb on his shooting hand and didn't tell me. He shot one for 14 the next night and we lost by five. My power forward, Adam, scored 18 points, ten above his average, and pulled down 15 rebounds. In the locker room after the game, I apologized to him in front of the team. I told him I had not coached him, or the others, properly. He could have been putting up those numbers all season if I hadn't limited his role. I had focused on the best player ON the team, not what was best FOR the team. I should have known better.

At the Yogi Berra Museum, thanks to Dave Kaplan, I have found some redemption. He's always told me how important it was for Yogi to be regarded as a good teammate. We now give a Best Teammate Award to one athlete from each of the schools that send their athletes, coaches or parents to our seminars. It's the best night of the year for us, and a bitter-sweet reminder for me.

Focus on the process, not the outcome.

Most coaches I know start out telling their team they're going to take things one game at a time. At the first practice they state that their goal is to get better every day through persistent effort. "If we work hard our record will take care of itself," has echoed off of the walls in every locker room in America. In that moment, as coaches, we wholeheartedly mean what we're saying. However, as the season progresses amnesia sets in. Suddenly, expectations change. "We're good enough to win our conference, county title, and state championship," replaces getting better every day through persistent effort. The goal somehow supersedes the process. I vividly remember getting sidetracked from my stated "one game at a time" intention during my first year coaching JV basketball at Montclair State College (MSC).

I was offered the position late in the summer of 1980. At the time I was living in Toms River, NJ, which is roughly 85 miles from the MSC campus. I jumped at the chance to coach on the college level despite the travel involved. Since I was hired late, I had no part in recruiting the players who would comprise my first college team. I met the 30 or so candidates in an auxiliary gym and introduced myself and my belief in taking it "one day at a time" philosophy. After two weeks, the roster was reduced to 15. These were now "my guys," even though I had nothing to do with recruiting them to MSC. There was obviously some talent, and with my deft handling of the personnel I thought we might have a good season.

Good turned to great quickly. Too quickly in fact. We ran off 10 straight wins against fairly stiff competition, including three Division 1 schools (MSC is a D3 school). The varsity was struggling at that point, so when Coach Gelston informed me that he was going to bring up my two captains to fill in as backups on the varsity I was disheartened. "One day at a time" was no longer on my radar. Going undefeated was the goal, to hell with the process. Thank goodness my players had a different mindset. They saw it as an opportunity for guys who had not been starters to show their ability and a chance for more guys to get playing time. I was too myopic to notice. We continued to play well, and though we were hard pressed to put some teams away, we remained unbeaten at 21-0 going into our final game. In the run up to that game, I spent the entire week stressing how this group had the chance to be the first undefeated team in the history of the school. If I said it once, I said it 50 times. I had forgotten that if they were smart enough to be admitted to college, they were smart enough to figure out that they hadn't lost any games at that point.

At Glassboro State, now Rowan, we met in the locker room for the last time that "my guys" would take the floor together. I was tighter than a sweater on a mannequin at Victoria Secret. Again, I reminded them of what was at stake. You know where this is going. We played our worst game of the season! Our points per game average of 70 was a distant shadow as we entered the final 1:26 in the second half down by five, 47-42. I called time-out. I tried to tell them they still had nearly a minute and a half to make things happen. No eye contact. I said, "Yes, your sneaker laces are tied! Pick your heads up and look at me. If we lose, it's my fault for putting too much pressure on you. Just don't give in to the situation." No reaction! Fortunately, a walk-on from Garfield, named John Ziemba, had no quit in him. In the final 1:26 he had two steals and scored six points. We won by a point and finished 22-0.

I got lucky that night and vowed never to place the outcome over the process again. I almost prevented these young men from accomplishing something very few athletes ever experience. My only salvation, in addition to John Ziemba, was that I had established such strong personal relationships with them off the court throughout the season that they would have forgiven me for clouding their thinking that night. At least that's what I need to believe.

Evan Ruggiero (left) joins me in reviewing the Coaches Dozen with Livingston High School athletes.

Conducting a workshop for captains and coaches from partnered SEC schools, Livingston High School and West Orange High School.

Speaking with a successful and significant coach, Ted Jarmusz, after his Monmouth Regional team won the state final. His teams have won several Umpires' Sportsmanship awards.

A great audience! The Lions from Mount St. Dominic Academy visit the museum for a fall sports kickoff assembly.

8 Takeaways for Coaches from Yogi

1. Be patient while players are developing.
2. Keep the game simple.
3. Stress fundamentals.
4. Display good sportsmanship.
5. Respect the game and the opponent.
6. Be honest with your players.
7. Play the game the right way. Don't cheat.
8. Never give up – "It ain't over til it's over."

8 Suggested Readings:

1. *A Season of Life* – Jeffrey Marx
2. *Sum it Up* – Pat Summitt
3. *Coaching Wisdom* – Mike Harrity
4. *Our Time* – Scott Iliano
5. *Chasing Perfect* – Bob Hurley
6. *They Call Me Coach* – John Wooden
7. *Leading With the Heart* – Coach Krzyzewski
8. *Top Dog: The Science of Winning and Losing* – Bronson and Ashley Merryman

8 Suggested Viewings:

1. *Coach Carter*
2. *Remember the Titans*
3. *Hoosiers*
4. *The Street Stops Here*
5. *Dead Poets' Society*
6. *Chariots of Fire*
7. *Vision Quest*
8. *Any Given Sunday*

Note to Coaches:

Don't stop reading now that you have your playbook for building a successful program and a possible significant career. The final part of this book is devoted to parents, specifically how they can assist, rather than impede you in your challenge. You won't get their support if you regard them as the enemy. They have a strong emotional connection to their son/daughter that sometimes gets the better of them. You need to keep that in mind as you reach out to them and ask them for their trust and their support. Try not to let a few negative voices drown out the sentiments of the less vocal majority. As Emerson wrote, "The faultfinders will find fault even in heaven."

I deliberately included instances where I made strategy errors while coaching to illustrate that I don't make any claim to know more about the science of coaching than you might. However, thanks to Russ Monica I learned what I needed to know about the art of coaching. I'm proud of the fact that over my three decade career as a coach I never publicly embarrassed a player, never gave up on a player and never forgot that I was a teacher first and foremost. The relationships I've developed with the hundreds of athletes I coached matter more to me than the records. Not a week goes by where I don't have some contact with a former player. That's the kind of paycheck I referred to earlier that keeps paying dividends. If you make the investment in your players' personal growth, equal to or above their athletic performance, you'll experience the same reward. That's a promise you can take to the bank.

Each year at Yogi's golf outing the crowd grows larger. Former players, coaches and celebrities fly in from all over the country just to see him and to make a donation to the Yogi Berra Museum. He's no longer their teammate or coach. They come because of how he made them feel, in some cases over 40, 50 years ago. Talk about a legacy!

Captains from Montclair Kimberly Academy and Montclair High School participate in a captain's workshop at the Museum.

Part 3 – Parents

"The best part about Little League is it keeps parents off the streets."

– Yogi Berra

The most important question for a parent: Do you enable or empower your child?

Former mayor of New York, Michael Bloomberg, stated that he got more nervous watching his daughter compete as an equestrian than he did running the city! Any parent who has sat in the bleachers watching a son or daughter compete can relate to that feeling. Being a parent is difficult. Being a sports parent is even harder. Dr. Gilbert jokingly refers to parents watching a game as experiencing "temporary insanity." All kidding aside, I believe the biggest threat to balancing the common ground of amateur athletics is the over-involved, over-zealous parent. "Helicopter" parents, as they are commonly referred to, have unfortunately advanced to "stealth bomber" status. Whatever their professed involvement ("I only want what's best for my kid."), they are unquestionably negatively altering youth sports.

It's true that there are misguided, self-serving, over-the-top coaches who have no business being involved with young athletes. They are equally responsible for 75% of kids dropping out of organized sports by the age of 13. School systems and recreation departments do their best to weed them out. Over the past few decades I've seen a reduction in their number.

However, my greatest fear is their number will increase if parental interference continues to drive quality coaches out of the profession. In my frequent interaction with coaches who attend our coaching seminars at the Yogi Berra Museum, I hear the same statement over and over: "I'm really considering getting out of coaching. I still like working with the kids, but I've had it with parents. They're a nightmare."

Over the course of my coaching career I had very few parental issues. I'd like to think it was because of my coaching style, but it probably was more about when I coached (in the 70's, 80's, and early 90's). So what's changed? Plenty! Rising college tuition, saturation of sports on TV, talk radio, AAU and travel teams, specialization, private coaching, social media, switching schools for athletic purposes – need more? How about the systematic elimination of childhood? We don't have kids anymore; we have mini-adults. In Florida there's a 4th grade girl currently playing on her high school basketball team. A New Jersey Division I coach was quoted as saying, "If you don't know who the best 7th graders are, you're not doing your job." This rapid acceleration of young athletes is the biggest threat to sports as Yogi and I knew them. Can it be stopped? I doubt it, but I do know that as a parent you don't have to get caught up in it.

Before I'm accused of being out of touch with current reality, or having "no skin in the game" because I don't have a child playing sports today, let me defend myself by saying that I do understand the bind parents feel they are in, and that I don't believe all parents are negative. However, I won't back off the statement that I made earlier that the negative ones are ruining the experience for everyone. The question for you, as a parent, is what are you communicating to your son/daughter about his/her participation on a team and his/her relationship with the coach? Are you enabling or empowering your son/daughter?

If you find yourself panicking over the prospect of navigating through the increasingly complex world of youth sports-relax. In the following pages, I will try to provide specific methods of coping with the pressure of doing what's best for your child/athlete. In the Appendix, I've included three op-ed pieces I wrote for the *Star-Ledger* a while back to show that for some time now I've been cognizant of the difficulty you face parenting an athlete. I hope you will take time to read them. Also, I urge you to step back for a moment and examine your thoughts and actions and ask yourself: "Am I a true 'booster' of my son's/daughter's team? Is my behavior having any negative impact on my son's/daughter's enjoyment of sports?" If you're not sure, take Dr. Gilbert's test, which I have also included in the Appendix.

Before I begin to identify specific strategies that will decrease your anxiety, let me relate how I came to understand the difference between enabling and empowering by telling you about three women from whom we can all learn.

Rob Gilbert (foreground), co-founder of the Institute for Coaching at YBM, is being introduced to the Caldwell HS Football team

Three Moms Who Empower

Ruth Ann Lobo —

One of Ruth's three children is a tall, lean, dynamic basketball star named Rebecca. In her senior year of high school, Rebecca received numerous college scholarship offers; she eventually chose to play at UConn under its firebrand coach, Gino Auriemma. At that time UConn was a program on the rise, but nowhere near the dominant position it now holds as one of the top women's basketball programs in the country. Auriemma was widely-known as a very demanding coach, too demanding some would argue. Still a taskmaster, he's mellowed somewhat while growing a program from relatively unknown to the pinnacle of women's sports. Rebecca Lobo got him started, though he nearly lost her before she ever played a game in a Huskie uniform.

During the pre-season of her freshman year, Rebecca grew very unhappy. She wasn't used to being consistently yelled at by a coach; basketball was no longer fun. She'd had it with Auriemma and decided to quit. She called home and told her mom, who supported her decision, but added one stipulation. She would come to UConn and bring Rebecca home only after Rebecca met with the coach and told him personally. Having a face to face with an intimidating coach was certainly not easy for the 18 year old freshman, but she knew her mother was serious. She met with Coach Auriemma the next day. He explained why he was pushing her so hard and shared his vision of what he saw in the program's future, including Rebecca's role in that future.

Rebecca remained at UConn and went on to earn All-American honors when UConn finished 35-0 in 1995 and won the NCAA title. Playing on the women's Olympic basketball team in 1996, she won a gold medal. Drafted by the New York Liberty in 1997, she spent seven seasons in the WNBA before moving on to a career in broadcasting. When asked what led to her success, Rebecca unhesitatingly responded that had her mother not forced her to take personal responsibility by talking to her coach, she would have left school. She's used that experience over the course of her career and it has made all the difference.

Ruth Ann Lobo, a school committee member in Southwick, MA, in the 80's and 90's was beloved in her community. In July of 2011, she lost a valiant battle with breast cancer. She had given Rebecca the gift of self-reliance, something all parents would do well to pass along to their children.

Debbie Phelps –

Debbie's son Michael was diagnosed with Attention Deficit Hyperactive Disorder (ADHD), at age 9. As a middle school principal at Windsor Mill School in Baltimore County, MD, she had some familiarity with the disorder and its accompanying behaviors. She knew behavior modification would be necessary. The youngest of three, two older sisters, Michael loved all sports, particularly swimming. Debbie supported his interest but required him to complete his homework before he could participate. She also made sure that he ate a healthy diet, providing food with less sugar.

Since Michael's disorder required constant monitoring, Debbie enlisted Michael's older sisters' support in watching what Michael ate and worked with her physician regulating his medication. Raising a child with ADHD is demanding, especially for someone who works as a full-time school administrator. The fact that Michael settled on swimming, with its early training hours and the travel involved for competition made Debbie's job much harder. She never wavered, even when Michael did.

My colleague, Rob Gilbert, tells the story of when he met Debbie Phelps. She was giving a talk at a bookstore in Princeton, NJ, and Rob decided to attend. After a brief talk about her role as an ADHD spokeswoman, she asked for questions. Rob was the first to raise his hand (he's always the first to do so) and asked her a great question: "Mrs. Phelps, was there ever a time when Michael didn't want to go to practice?" Her response was right out of the Ruth Ann Lobo Playbook. "Are you kidding? All the time," she replied. "I finally stopped him from whining one morning. I had gotten up at 5 am, prepared his breakfast and went outside to warm up the car. Michael opened his window and called down to me, 'Ma, I don't wanna go to practice today.' I told him, no problem Michael, you just have to call the coach and let him know. I would have been fine had he done it. It was his decision to make, not mine."

Michael went on to become the most decorated swimmer of all time, with a total of 22 medals (18 Olympic gold). He was recognized as the World Swimmer of the Year seven times and the US Swimmer of the year nine times. He has continued to train while focusing on a foundation he started in 2008, which aims at growing the sport of swimming while promoting healthier lifestyles.

Debbie Phelps, once recognized by Johnson and Johnson as "Mom of the Olympics," is currently active in ADHD Moms, an online community and resource for mothers of children with the condition.

Pat Summitt —

It couldn't have been easy for Ross Summitt growing up as an only child, especially when his mother is probably the most recognizable person in the state of Tennessee. Raised on a farm, with brothers who forced her to become fiercely competitive, Pat Summitt knew a lot about hard work. Just because she was a female didn't excuse her from performing all of the backbreaking chores her father assigned. Her brothers never took it easy on her when they had scant free time from chores and school to play basketball. It's no wonder her work ethic and competitive spirit took her from the farm to the Hall of Fame in 2000.

One night, after a long day in her office and a grueling practice, Coach Summitt arrived home to find her son lying on his bed crying. When she asked him why he was upset, he told her that he had been cut from his high school basketball team. She calmly asked, "Are you crying because you got cut or because you didn't work hard enough to make the team? You see that new basketball over there in the corner? When you wear out the threads on it practicing you won't have to cry about not making the team."

Sound insensitive? As the winningest basketball coach, male or female, (1,098 victories, eight national titles, and an Olympic gold medal), she could have called the school and complained to the principal or the AD. As highly regarded as she was, she could have gotten Ross reinstated, even if it meant firing the coach. She didn't. She was trying to teach her son that if he wanted something in his life he had to go out and work hard to earn it.

Coach Summitt might have a steely glare and will never be mistaken for soft, but that doesn't mean she isn't kind-hearted and caring. Her players love her. She was demanding, yet many regard her as a second mother. Her 100% graduation rate is a testament to her concern for her female charges. After a divorce, she raised Ross by herself. Though he was her "baby," she never babied him. No one could ever question her devotion to him. There isn't a single picture of a Tennessee basketball celebration, and there were many, where Ross isn't in Pat's arms or standing beside her.

Ross went on to graduate from the University and continues to be a fixture at all Lady Vol's games. He didn't take that new basketball and become the next Michael Jordan, but he did learn that what you do, not who you are, is what really matters.

Pat Summitt was awarded the Presidential Medal of Freedom in 2012 by President Obama. Unfortunately, she developed an early onset of dementia and decided to retire from coaching. She lends her name to foundations fighting the disease and helps raise funds for research. Coach Summitt and Ross still attend Lady Vol's home games, only now they sit across from the team rather than next to it.

The course of action these three women took remind me of something Bill Walton, former UCLA great and NBA Hall of Famer wrote: "No matter how hard we try and how desperately we want the best for our children, the only way that someone is going to be truly great at anything is if they want to get there themselves. The worst things you can do for the ones you love are the things that they could or should do for themselves."

Our kids want us to listen to their problems, not solve them. They need to fight their own battles to become their own advocates. We need to empower them, not enable them.

The Parent's Dozen

1. Place your child's wishes before your own.

Kids want to have fun playing sports with their friends. Parents want scholarships. These goals are bound to clash. It's true that there's some overlap. Most parents want their kids to enjoy their sports experience, and what kid wouldn't be thrilled to be offered a college scholarship? The reality is that there's a much greater likelihood that the student/athlete will enjoy his/her participation without the pressure of knowing his/her parents are fixated on that scholarship. It's worth noting that there is $1 billion available in athletic scholarships each year. That sounds like a lot until you consider that there's $22 billion available in academic scholarships each year! Perhaps a math tutor could be a better investment than a pitching coach?

With college costs skyrocketing, it's certainly understandable why all parents would love financial assistance, especially if their son/daughter is a gifted athlete. The problem is the numbers are against them. There are roughly 41 million below college-age athletes. Of that number, only 360,000 make a college team.

Most parents aren't aware that there is no such thing as a full, four-year scholarship. The scholarship is for one year and must be renewed. While it's not a good practice to rescind a scholarship, it's done regularly. Additionally, with the exception of football and basketball, not all athletes on a college team receive scholarship money. Soccer, for instance, has only nine scholarships available per year, volleyball 11 and baseball 13. The funds are sometimes amortized over the total number of athletes on the team.

Some athletes on Division I and Division II teams receive no financial support other than loans. In Division III, there are no scholarships. (For further amplification, I've included statistics about scholarships in the Appendix.)

If we recognize that of the 900,000 young men who play high school football, only 6% will make a college team, and less than 2% of that group will make the NFL, most parents will need a Plan B. You might be lucky enough to have a truly elite athletic son/daughter; most of us don't. Our job then, it seems to me, is to be less myopic about scholarships and just be our kids' biggest fans. We need to encourage and support them regardless of how much they play or how well they play, knowing that playing for their high school team may be their last experience on a team. The memories they make playing with their friends will last a lifetime.

The advice Yogi gives to the youngsters who come to the summer baseball camp offered at the Museum is always the same: "Have fun and don't get mad at anybody." That philosophy carried him from the sandlot in St. Louis to the Baseball Hall of Fame.

2. Let your athletes learn at their own pace.

Playing sports at a young age is important for several reasons. Sports provide social interaction, a chance to build self-confidence and communication skills, and perhaps most importantly, require physical exertion. It's not hard to understand that sitting on a couch playing Xbox doesn't contribute to a healthy lifestyle. The number of cases of childhood obesity is alarming; that's why it's important to get kids moving early. The problem is once we get them moving, we move them too fast. Everything is too structured, too adult-driven. Tee-ball wasn't enough. Now we have Tee-ball tournaments, and third grade traveling team soccer championships.

These weren't created by kids – adults decided they were necessary in order to get kids ready for a competitive life. No wonder the majority of kids drop out of organized sports before they turn 13. We're taking their fun away. We need to change our thinking-fast.

Trying anything new is difficult, especially when a youngster's body isn't fully developed. What parents and coaches need to do is encourage effort instead of praising results. "Nice try, Johnny," will have a longer impact than "Great catch, Johnny," because Johnny might not catch the next ball, but he certainly can continue to try hard. It's human nature for a parent to feel and express pride when their child accomplishes something athletically. "That's my kid, and he's a great athlete!" is fine; better still would be,"That's my great kid, and he's becoming an athlete."

Studies show that younger kids perform better when they practice without parents around and are continually encouraged for making progress. They can only handle criticism when they are older and have achieved some level of competence. Only then can they play before a crowd. The key is not to rush them and to remain positive. Let kids know that 'this' (their sport) is their thing, not ours. Not being around them also helps them become more independent. There's no need for parents to go to every game. Kids need room to fail. They don't need to come home and watch their mistakes on TV because dad filmed the game. If you find that you have to be at a practice, sit far away reading a book, and then drive your son/daughter home. Otherwise, there is no need to be present at a practice. Your youngster won't tell you not to come around all the time. When they visit the YBM, they ask me to tell you. So, I'm telling you for them: Give them space to grow.

We can learn a lot from Sara Blakely's father. When Sara came home from a tryout and informed her father that she didn't make the team he gave her a High Five! How many of us would do that? What he was saying to her was, "I'm glad you're trying new things. You won't always succeed, but don't stop trying." She went on to fail the LSATs, was turned down repeatedly for loans for a business idea, and yet she never gave up. She is now the first self-made female billionaire and the CEO of Spanx. You might have the next Sara Blakely in your house. You'll never know if you don't teach him/her that failure isn't fatal or permanent. A setback is just a setup for a comeback.

3. Emphasize academics and a balanced school record.

You don't want your child to wait until midway through high school to build a transcript that is balanced enough to gain admittance to college. Academics must be the first priority. If you feel your son/daughter is lacking in study skills, you need to address that immediately. Many kids see school as a burden, something to occupy their time until practice begins. Our task as parents is to help them understand that they are a thousand times more likely to go to college than the pros, and they can't wait until their junior or senior years to realize that. Staying on their back about their homework and studying for tests won't make you their best friend, but you're not their best friend; you're their parent.

In my 34 year career teaching high school English and Speech, I had countless students come to me in their senior year and express regret for not taking anything but sports seriously. They had low grades, no participation in clubs or activities and no community service. Their transcript listed Football 1, 2, 3, 4.

They didn't even play another sport! As a coach, I've had far too many recruiters tell me, "He'd fit in well in our program. We really like him, but I can't get him in with his transcript." Don't let a recruiter say that about your son or daughter. Start early and stay on them.

Encourage your child to participate in multiple sports. Ask them which clubs or organizations they would like to join, not if they want to join. Find a community service activity you can participate in with him/her. It will do you both some good and show how committed you are to helping them see a world beyond themselves, beyond sports. Colleges want well-rounded students.

If you find yourself in a position where your son/daughter has little or no chance of gaining admittance to a four-year college, investigate the community colleges in your area. The academic profiles of the two-year schools have steadily improved over the past decade. In fact, many two-year schools have partnered with four-year state universities and have arranged for acceptance of their students who earn an Associate Degree. These schools are considerably more affordable and offer a number of intercollegiate sports. This might not be the path you envisioned for your son/daughter, but not all journeys follow a straight road. The key is to find the "right" school, not the best school.

There are $1 billion in athletic scholarships available each year. There are $22 billion in academic scholarships available each year. Maybe a math or English tutor is worth more than a pitching coach?

---

4. Avoid early specialization.

Sociologists have surmised that parents feel compelled to nurture every minor skill their kids demonstrate. That mindset suggests that kids can't be just average happy-go-lucky kids anymore. Where has this thinking gotten us? "Gifted and Talented" summer programs for second graders. Really? "Proud Parent of a Middle School Honor Student". What happens when the 11-year-old doesn't make the honor roll next term? No longer proud?

Every parent is entitled to think their kids are special. The danger lies in limiting a child to laser-like focus on a particular interest, aptitude or physical skill that a child demonstrates early on. Yes, I have heard of Tiger Woods and Michael Phelps. Who is the second Tiger? Phelps? They're one in a million athletic specimens. My point is most kids aren't elite athletes; most will not play a sport beyond high school. That's not a knock – it's reality. Check the figures in the appendix if you're not convinced.

Is there a time when specialization is a good idea? Most coaches would suggest that athletes participate in multiple sports until their junior year. The one exception might be girls soccer, which begins Olympic programs early in high school. Some of these girls are being recruited off of club teams as early as eighth grade by college coaches who think it's wrong on many levels, but do it so as not to lose out on the top players. The college recruiters I've worked with over the past quarter century tell me they prefer athletes who play more than one sport. They believe doing so provides greater opportunities to compete and limits the risk of injury due to repetitive motion. Dr. James Andrews, the noted orthopedic surgeon, is alarmed by the number of Tommy John surgeries he's now performing on teenagers.

Another downside of early specialization is that it limits a youngster's social interaction to the same group of people, including coaches. What if something unforeseen happens, a debilitating injury? A forced relocation? These are very real possibilities. The more involved an individual is the greater exposure to people with different backgrounds and interests, the larger the pool from which to draw friends, the more exposure to different motivational and coaching styles.

Have there been parents who, led by a persuasive coach or the lure of a scholarship, have seen their child benefit from specializing in one sport? Sure. Their stories, though, are few and far between. More often than not, it ends poorly. Consider the couple who were told their five-year-old son was a "can't miss" tennis star. They moved their family of five to France from California so he could receive special coaching from a renowned tennis guru for $140,000 a year. At first the budding star responded well to coaching and won tournaments for his age group. However, the grind of hours of practice and intensity of competition took its toll. He felt burned out and announced that he no longer wanted to pursue a professional career. Game, set, match. His parents had sold their home, quit their jobs, spent their savings, and taken their kids out of their schools. You're not surprised they're contemplating divorce, are you? Is this an extreme case or a cautionary tale? You decide, and when you decide on early specialization for your youngster, ask yourself this question: Is that what my son/daughter wants, or what I want?

When a pro scout told Yogi that his son, Dale, would be a first round draft choice in baseball if he gave up hockey in high school, Yogi said, "He likes hockey! He can decide to play it if he wants to." Dale did play hockey. He went on to play nine years in major league baseball.

5. Let your kids decide.

Years ago I attended a "Sports Nut Night" sponsored by the Football Hall of Fame. Each table was given 100 sports trivia questions and half an hour to complete them. The questions covered football, basketball, baseball, hockey, tennis and horse racing. The table with the most correct answers got the best prizes. My table got umbrellas – we knew nothing about hockey or horse racing.

While the answer sheets were being checked, the committee introduced a panel of writers and athletes who would answer questions. It was quite a panel: Jerry Izenberg, from the NJ *Star Ledger*; Bill Madden, from the *Daily News*; Bert Sugar, from *Ring Magazine*; Frank Tripuka, former Notre Dame and Denver Bronco star; and Yogi Berra. The back and forth was spirited and enlightening. One question in particular caught my attention, and it has become the gold standard I use whenever I speak to parents. The conversation went like this:

> **Questioner: "Yogi, my son told me he wants to get a pitching coach for his son. Is that a good idea?"**
>
> **Yogi: "How old is the kid?"**
>
> **Questioner: "Nine."**
>
> **Yogi: "How the hell do you know if he's any good? Gee whiz – he's only nine!"**
>
> **Questioner: "That's what I told my son, but he still wants to do it. What should I tell him?"**
>
> **Yogi: "What does the kid want?"**

There you have it. In the simplest terms, Yogi, once again, proved to be a sage. No wonder he is the most quoted individual at graduation ceremonies. He has a unique ability to reduce anything to its core. He certainly did that night.

As hard as it is to accept that our kids don't always think like we do, life forces us to face that reality. There's a great video I'd like you to check out on YouTube. Look for "Philly Fan Catches Foul Ball, Gives it to Daughter." You'll see a young father, obviously a big Philadelphia Phillies fan, as indicated by the tee shirt and cap he's wearing. A Phillies batter fouls off a pitch into the first row of the second deck behind the Phillies' dugout. The father catches it, his first-ever souvenir after many trips to the stadium. He raises his arms in triumph so all fans can celebrate the acquisition of his keepsake from his beloved team. Bursting with pride, he hands the ball to his six-year-old daughter, who promptly releases the ball and lets it fall. The father, crestfallen though he may be, picks her up and hugs her. What a metaphor for parents – and very consistent with Yogi's mentality. Our kids won't always share our passion. However, no matter what they do, they're still our kids. Our only job is to love them.

Whatever your kids want to do, you need to support them. You have to let them make their decisions on what they want to pursue because they're the ones who have to put the work in. Imagine if Evan Ruggiero's father had pushed him to continue to play baseball instead of supporting Evan's decision to dance. What would their relationship have been like when Evan needed his support to fight the cancer which ultimately cost him his leg?

6. Teach the concept of "sweat equity."

Emerson wrote, "Nothing great was ever accomplished without enthusiasm." Edison wrote, "Genius is 1% inspiration and 99% perspiration." Those men were prophets for everyone who has ever accomplished anything, including sports. As Coyle wrote in *The Talent Code*, we mistakenly believe that individuals are born talented. As a result, we suffer from what some refer to as the "iceberg effect." That is, we see a performance without thinking of the underlying effort that went into it.

Turn on the television at seven o'clock and watch Derek Jeter make a backhand stab in the hole, set his feet and fire to first in time to nip a runner. Watch Ray Allen drain a three-pointer from the top of the circle. What we don't see, and probably don't give any thought to, is Jeter fielding 200 ground balls from 5:00-5:30, before he takes batting practice, or Ray Allen firing up 50 shots from one spot, then moving to several spots and working on his catch and release three hours before tipoff. The best athletes are always the hardest workers. These days they're also required to perform rigorous off-season workouts. Top athletes don't just show up and star when the lights come on. Their secret, which is really no secret at all, is anyone who wants to perform well must devote an extraordinary number of hours to deliberate practice.

If it is true that "anything worth doing is worth doing well," we need to explain to our sons/daughters that success in whatever sport(s) they choose to play, requires that they make a serious time commitment to work on fundamentals and learn the game(s) inside out. This will only occur, as Yogi suggested, if the kid, not his dad, really wants it to occur.

K. Anders Ericcson, a professor at Florida State, is often referred to as "the" expert on performance. His belief is that mastery occurs only after 10,000 hours. I reference his finding, not to discourage you, but to provide context. Certainly young athletes can't be expected to reach mastery. The task, then, is to convince them that they can be anything they want to be if they're willing to put forth the effort. As Vince Lombardi said, "The will to win isn't as important as the will to prepare." His philosophy was definitely embraced by his players. Getting today's kids to buy into it is more challenging, but worth the effort. It's applicable to their lives, not just their athletic careers.

Technology has brought the world to teenagers' fingertips-literally. There's no need to travel to a library to access information. A few finger taps on an iPad or smart phone provides instant results. Remember those stories your parents and grandparents told you about having to walk miles to school, uphill both ways? Today's kids don't walk anywhere. You chauffer them, or they have their own car. Are all kids spoiled? Many are. Are yours? When the work gets hard, do they give up? Many do. Do yours?

Please don't get me wrong, I think kids are great! However, I also think many are lazy. During our talks to athletes at YBM, we try our best to sell the idea that we believe they can do great things if they are willing to work hard. We use Yogi as an example. He didn't possess the physicality of most of his professional peers. His hard work made up for whatever he lacked. "Sweat equity" earned him the distinction of being named one of the top 50 players of all time.

7. Watch out for "cash cows."

On the last basketball team I coached, I had a 6'8" forward who wasn't much of an athlete (bad hands, low basketball IQ, poor work ethic). Having listened to coaches at clinics over the years who said, "You can't teach size," I kept him. I knew he couldn't really help us, but I thought it would be a good experience for him. Before the season started, I began receiving letters from college coaches expressing interest in him. My first thought was that I was being "pranked" by my associate coach. He was as dumbfounded as I was and couldn't contain his laughter. A steady stream of letters continued; I passed them along without comment.

Through no concerted effort on our part, we learned that the young man had attended a summer camp, run by a friend of his dad. As a favor, he submitted the young man's name to a scouting service. Letter after letter continued to arrive from coaches who had never seen this kid play, inviting him for an unofficial visit. I was never consulted. The letters were placed in my mailbox at school and I hand-delivered them to a 6'8" forward who was so afraid of failure he quit the team at half-time during our third game - a game he started! We did nothing but encourage him. He knew his limitations. He didn't want to be exposed publically, so he quit.

I don't have to tell you that sports are a big business in this country. There are nearly as many scouting services and Amateur Athletic Union (AAU) teams as there are colleges. Some are credible, most are not. Sifting through them can be a daunting task, and we can expect to see more of them in the future. College coaches have not hidden their disdain for these for-profit organizations. They much prefer to deal directly with high school coaches, but the sports landscape has changed, so they play along.

As a parent, it's easy to be taken in by an AAU coach or camp director who promises to get your son/daughter exposure to coaches offering scholarships. They cite a few success stories and create the illusion that they can do the same thing for your "can't miss" athlete. Trust me, in the end it's about money, always about money. I could write a book about these scam artists, but others have already done that, and better than I could. (Read *Play Their Hearts Out* by George Dohrmann). College campuses, once ghost towns during the summer, are now dotted with future 'pros' running around in one-size fits all tee shirts. If you're looking for glorified baby-sitting, you've arrived at the right place.

Enough doom and gloom. Are there good programs for athletes during the summer? Absolutely. How do you find them, and what should you look for in a camp? That first place to start is with your coaches at school. They know your son/daughter and can find the right fit. If you aren't comfortable with a particular coach, ask the AD for a recommendation. You might also ask other parents if they have any experience with camps or summer leagues. Take their advice with reservation. Unlike the shirts handed out at camp, one size doesn't fit all. Take a closer look at the program online. What's the counselor/camper ratio? What is the experience level of the staff? How much time is devoted to individual instruction and emphasis on fundamentals compared to games? How does the cost compare with what someone you trust locally will charge for private instruction? Does the camp brochure promise appearances by pro athletes? Don't be duped. Getting to watch a pro do a drill and getting an autograph won't make your son/daughter a better player.

One additional suggestion: For a high school athlete who has some idea where he/she would like to attend college, it's good to go to a camp on that campus if it's run by the coaching staff. This works for Division I as well as Division II and Division III. The coaches get an extended look at your son/daughter and can determine if they can compete at their school. Your youngster gets a feel for the campus and a chance to see what the coaches are like. I've known of several students/athletes who have taken this approach and been rewarded.

I'm not trying to make you distrustful of everyone. My intention is merely to remind you of the number one rule in business: Let the buyer beware. Before you make an investment in your son's/daughter's athletic future, do your homework. There's nothing better than investing in kids, especially when it's done wisely.

8. Let coaches coach.

I know, you've heard this before, but if you're still reading, either you believe I'm trying to help you make good decisions concerning your son's/daughter's sports experience, or I owe you money. I hope it's the former. If it is, bear with me a little longer, and I'll try to merit your time. If it's the latter, tell your friends to buy this book so I can pay you back.

Full disclosure – I haven't coached in over a decade. However, no one I know has spent more time talking to athletes and coaches, or watching games, than I have since I co-founded the Institute for Coaching at YBM in 2006. Additionally, I teach Coaching Principles/Problems at Montclair State University and attend an average of four high school and/or college games per week. I enjoy the action, but most of my attention is on the coach and on the spectators. How the coach interacts with players, officials, the press and parents is my main concern. Here's what I've learned and what they tell me:

While some coaches over-coach and occasionally lose their composure, the overwhelming number of coaches are knowledgeable, well-prepared and care about their players.

Coaching has become a year-round job. Monitoring grades, supervising out-of-season conditioning, observing feeder programs, working with recruiters, meeting district professional development demands, watching film and preparing a budget and a schedule are some, but not all, of their job requirements.

All coaches want to win. They will play the individuals who give them the best chance to win. They don't limit the playing time of individuals they don't like, regardless of what some athletes or parents think. Please read the previous sentence again. It's fair to question a coach's decisions, but unfair to question his/her motivation.

Improvement in technology is a mixed blessing. Hudl has made it possible for coaches to prepare cuts of game film which can be sent to college recruiters. It's also easier to scout opponents. Web pages facilitate communicating with athletes and parents. On the downside, coaches need to monitor their athletes' use of social media. Internet bullying and trash talking have become pervasive among high school and college athletes.

The pressure on coaches is more intense than ever. When they win, they don't dominate enough. When they lose, they got outcoached. Dot coms allow anonymous critics to rip coaches with impunity. Parents complain their kid doesn't play enough. If he/she is a starter, he/she isn't featured enough, or isn't getting enough attention from college recruiters.

The number one reason good coaches leave the profession? Over-involved, over-indulgent parents.

Do I have a bias toward coaches? Absolutely. Am I concerned because good coaches I meet are ready to give it up? Yes. Re-read the last few paragraphs and ask yourself: Would I want the job? I'm not sure I could coach under these conditions.

My question to you is, are you making your son's/daughter's coach's job more difficult? Do you support the coach publicly? Privately? Do you criticize the coach in front of your son/daughter? Do you think that helps? Let me close this section with some advice from *The Encyclopedia of Sports Parenting:*

On matters of playing time and strategy, stay out of it.

On matters of health and ethics, you're certainly within your rights.

Your job is to counsel your child, not ride in on a big white horse and take care of him/her.

I've heard Yogi give the same advice. I don't know a single coach who would disagree. In Part 2–Coaches, I wrote that coaches get paychecks, that aren't available in any other profession. For your kid's sake, be a dividend, not a withdrawal.

On matters of playing time and strategy, stay out. On matters of health and ethics, you're certainly within your rights.

-The Encyclopedia of Sports Parenting

---

9. Avoid PGA's.

Several years ago a Stanford University study asked athletes from tee-ball through college to respond to the following question: What do you like least about sports? A staggering 75% of the respondents gave the same answer (I used the word "staggering" because I don't know of any other poll result where 75% responded with the identical answer): Three quarters of the age 5-22 athletes reported that the thing they like least about playing a sport is the PGA (Post Game Analysis) by their parents. After a game, kids want to know one thing: "Where are we going to eat?"

Here's a comment made by a recent student of mine at MSU: "My mom is the queen of the PGA. She doesn't know much about softball, but as soon as I get into the car, she starts to correct my mistakes. Usually what she says I should do is the opposite of what my coach tells me. I love my mom, but sometimes I wish she'd keep her comments to herself, especially after a loss when I'm in no mood to talk about the game."

I raise this issue whenever I give a talk at YBM for parents. Invariably, after the session ends, someone will come up to me and say, "I never knew that a PGA, as you call it, bothered my son. I'm kind of embarrassed. I do it all the time." My response is, "Well, now you know. Maybe you should just say, 'I really enjoy watching you play. Are you hungry?'"

Kids don't want to hear what it was like when you played. They'll roll their eyes, and put on their headphones. Your criticism of the coach, or the officials for that matter, is irrelevant because a player has no control over either. They don't decide who plays or how much they play. If they didn't play well, or played very little, they may feel that they're disappointing you. If there is some discussion of the game on the ride home, let your son/daughter initiate it.

At this point I'm reminded of what another parent shared with me at YBM after a talk I gave on "Transitioning Your Eighth Grader to High School Sports." As I mentioned before, kids need room to fail. That's how they learn. They don't need someone (especially not a parent) critiquing their every move. They also don't need a video chronicling their mistakes. During my talk I stated, "You don't have to go to every game. In fact, it's probably better if you don't. Maybe you can just attend home games." When I finished speaking, a woman came up to me and said, "I really have to thank you. I was feeling guilty whenever I missed one of my son's games." My response was, "You don't need permission to miss games. Remember, this is 'his thing,' not yours."

When Yogi's three sons were growing up, he was usually squatting behind the plate at Yankee Stadium. He saw them play when he could. Despite his absence, they each managed to achieve success. Larry played in the Mets organization and became a lifelong competitive softball player. Tim played for the Baltimore Colts, and Dale had a solid career with the Pittsburgh Pirates and New York Yankees. Yogi didn't have to be ever-present to support them. He let their coaches do the coaching. He "schooled" them on the golf course.

> The best thing any parent can say after a game is "I love watching you play."

10. "Chill out" during games.

I'm going out on a limb here, but I'm guessing you've heard this before. Let me offer you a few reasons you might not be aware of as to why being calm at a game is important:

Silent recruiting – Many coaches go to games to watch how a recruit competes. There's only so much that can be gleaned from watching videotapes. They don't wear any clothing that identifies their college affiliation. They try to blend in with the crowd. Their primary goal is to see how a prospect handles a setback. They look closely at body language and check to see if the prospect scans the stands looking for his parents. Speaking of parents in the stands, coaches watch a recruit's parents as well. Are they vocal? Do they yell at officials and/or coaches? The phrase I've heard, which explains why they recruit in this manner, is "Nobody wants to dance with somebody else's devil." Furthermore, coaches tell me that all recruiters ask them the same three questions: "How are his/her grades? What kind of kid is he/she? Are the parents a pain in the ass?" Coaches will settle for a kid with lesser talent if it frees them from having to deal with problematic parents.

$P = P - I - I$ went into great detail on this concept in the section devoted to athletes. In sum, it's a formula related to an athlete's performance (Your Performance is equal to your Potential, Minus Interference.) Athletes are trained to hear one voice - their coach's. Any other voice creates a distraction. The people who shout instructions from the stands are just adding noise (interference) and pressure. Encouragement through clapping and cheering can most certainly produce an increase in an athlete's energy level, which in turn, may have a positive impact on his/her performance. However, the truth is, unless a crowd is sparse, players can't hear what's being said. They've become skilled at tuning it out. So while it may serve as a release of pent up anxiety or frustration for parents to constantly shout instructions, it's far more likely that they annoy everyone sitting around them than they help their youngster.

Providing a Window - Every school has an honor society, a choir, a drama program and a host of other activities which make them proud. Trouble is, most non-residents like me, never see the signature events put on by these organizations. We don't see your NHS Induction, Winter Concert or Spring Musical. Our only view into your son's/daughter's school is their sports program. While it's certainly not fair of us to judge your school solely by observing how its teams and spectators behave, we do. It's our only prism, and unfortunately we share our opinion, regardless of whether it's accurate. Knowing that I might be in attendance at one of your athletic events someday, how would you like me to describe my experience to other non-residents?

"I went to a game yesterday in <u>your town</u> and I couldn't believe how nasty the people were. Their players did nothing but trash talk. Their coaches complained about every call, and their fans were obnoxious. They booed the visiting team and the refs, and they held up mocking signs. I was really uncomfortable. I'm glad I don't live there."

"I went to a game yesterday in <u>your town</u>. I couldn't believe how nice everyone was. The ticket-takers said, "Welcome to <u>your town</u>, thanks for coming. Enjoy the game." They gave me a free printout of the rosters. Their players helped up opponents who fell. Their coaches spent time greeting the opposing coaches and seemed to be joking with the refs. Their fans cheered just as hard when they were behind as when they were ahead. They even clapped for the visiting team's cheerleaders. I was really comfortable there. I'll probably go back."

Maybe you're proud of your town, and you don't care what I, or any other non-resident, thinks about it. That's your prerogative. One thing you might consider though is property value. Often a choice to buy or not comes down to the reputation of the town and its schools. Additionally, your son/daughter might seek employment outside his/her community. The people doing the hiring might be more inclined to hire him/her if they have a favorable view of your town. It certainly can't hurt.

*The op-ed, "You're Perfectly Entitled to Think It, Just Don't Say It," which appears in the Appendix, will hopefully be more illuminating.

11. Become a booster who actually 'boosts.'

Years ago I was standing along the shoreline in Seaside Park, New Jersey, when a woman I recognized as a graduate of the same high school I attended came over to say hello. While we talked, we were joined by a woman, Sue, whom I didn't know. What she said still bothers me. "Pat," she said, "I just heard you're running for the Board of Ed. Wow, you realize how much power you're going to have? You can pick your kids' teachers, and if you don't like any of Mike's coaches, you can get them fired. I really envy you."

Before I could hear Pat's response, I did a header into the freezing surf. Call me naïve, or stupid, for that matter, but I never considered that a parent's primary motivation for running for the Board of Education was to engineer her kids' academic and athletic experience. Fortunately, Pat had altruistic goals. I taught three of her kids, and she was very supportive. She also served on the Booster Club for several years and was highly respected throughout the community. Unfortunately, these days I'm hearing about more Sues than Pats. Many more parents are volunteering because they hope to engender favor with their kids' coaches and gain a voice with the athletic administration. No wonder the running joke is that the best job in America is Athletic Director at an orphanage. Haven't heard that one? I'm not surprised – no one looking to remain employed would say it out loud. I'll say it for them.

Do people like Pat still join the Booster Club? Absolutely. I see them running the snack bar, arranging banquets, taking ads in the yearbook and organizing and working Project Graduation. They devote hours, anonymously laboring to provide their kids with the most positive athletic experience possible. These are remarkable, selfless individuals whom I greatly respect. We need more people like them. What we don't need, just like we don't need self-serving coaches, is "boosters" who only boost their agenda. Ego-driven coaches and power-driven boosters are a cancer in youth sports, and like a real-life cancer, if they can't be treated, they need to be removed.

As if great boosters don't do enough, I'd like to see them do one more thing: involve themselves and their student/athletes in community service. Not merely community service that satisfies a high school graduation requirement, but something which teaches youngsters that there's nothing that feels better than doing something for others, especially those who can't do things for themselves. We're at our best when we demonstrate our humanity.

Whether or not people follow sports, they know the inspirational story of Jackie Robinson. However, not many know the quiet struggle of the second individual who broke the color barrier, Paterson, NJ, native Larry Doby. Doby experienced the same bigotry Robinson faced, without any of the fanfare. One of his biggest supporters during his career was Yogi. In fact, Doby would visit the Museum to speak to students until he died in 2003, and the Museum ran summer baseball and softball camps for kids in Doby's hometown of Paterson, NJ. Yogi watches from the terrace overlooking the stadium, named in his honor, and smiles. He lends his name to anything that lifts others. As a booster, you can do the same by lifting your athletic program to new heights. Hold this thought: A candle loses nothing by lighting another.

12. Empower, instead of enabling.

Pick up any current magazine, and you're bound to find an article on the pampered, over-indulged child. What forces are at work that have brought about such frequent criticism of child-rearing? Is this fair? Accurate? I'm not sure, but I do believe it is more important than ever that kids learn to become self-reliant. They face significantly more challenges than we did a generation ago, and we can't always be there to hold their hand and make decisions for them. Our job is to help them become their own advocate.

Our first step is to quit trying to be the "Happiness Police." When we were growing up, our parents were only concerned with two things: our safety and providing us with a chance for a better life than they had. Our education was paramount. Somewhere along the way, a new generation of parents decided that their role was to ensure the happiness of their offspring. If their kids were happy, they must be doing a good job as a parent. The problem with that mindset is happiness is fleeting, and it can't be engineered through play group, Gymboree, or a full schedule of activities we select for them.

Exposing kids to a variety of activities is, in and of itself, a good idea. However, kids need to find their own way. They need some unstructured "down time." As they grow, they usually settle into a routine centered on things they enjoy doing. It has to be their choice. If it's not, they won't put in the time or the effort to become good enough at it to keep them engaged.

Once a youngster decides what he/she really enjoys doing, he/she has to own it. It it's a sport, he/she needs to make sure all necessary equipment is at the ready, all practice times and game times are written down, and consideration has been given to arriving early. If parents pack the gear and the Gatorade and have to remind their kids about practice time, kids will never do things for themselves. Better they should show up late and/or missing equipment and have to face the coach. Usually it won't happen a second time.

As I mentioned in the section on Athletes, we had one rule when I coached basketball at Montclair State: Be at the right place, at the right time, and do the right thing. It's never too early to introduce this concept to kids. The beauty of the rule is it places responsibility on the athlete to think. Where am I supposed to be? When do I have to be there? Is this something I should be doing? I'm not suggesting you throw your non-swimmer into the pool and say "swim." You need to use water wings until he/she realizes they can swim without any aid. Our role as parents is to make suggestions and let our kids make decisions. They may grouse about a situation they face, but they're merely engaging in "troubles talk." For the most part, they don't want us to tell them what they should do; they just want us to listen.

I learned this the hard way when my daughter was 13. After a courageous two-year battle against breast cancer, my wife, Pam, died. My daughter, Erin, was in eighth grade. We muddled through the year doing everyday things that previously had been done for us. We didn't talk much about our painful loss. The first day of school the following September, Erin was sitting in her last period class, 9th grade math, when a voice came over the PA summoning her to the social services office. What kid wants to be called to that office on her first day at a new school? When I got home from my school, she told me what had happened. In a relatively calm voice, she informed me that the social worker had called her in and asked her several questions: "How does it feel entering an empty house after school? Are you lonely on holidays? Is your father seeing anyone?" I don't think I heard the rest – my anger was deafening.

As a male with a Type A personality, I was incensed. I rattled off my questions, machine-gun style. "Who is this person? Where is her office? Why would she call you down?" As soon as I announced that I'd be at the counselor's office first thing the next morning, my daughter ran to her room and cried for hours. Later she went into the shower and cried there. It became obvious that my over-reaction had really upset her. We didn't talk for two days. The third day she was sitting in the living room when I arrived home. She told me that the Student Assistance Counselor had called her down to his office to ask her how she was doing. He told her about a group he had formed for students who had lost a parent or grandparent and asked her if she'd like to join.

Aware of the previous mess I had made just two days ago, I bit my tongue and said, "How did that make you feel?" She replied, "Not too good, but you and I are doing better."

It was a seminal moment for me. All she had wanted was for me to listen. She would handle her own business. My 13-year-old had acted more maturely than I had. It was a lesson I've never forgotten. As I write this she is 31 and in her tenth year teaching third grade. She still engages me in "troubles talk." Only now I make suggestions; she makes decisions. Works for me – I know it will work for you.

When your youngster comes home complaining about a teacher or a coach, just listen. Suggest that he/she make an appointment to speak privately to him/her and to express concerns openly and honestly. You might have an impulse to call the teacher or coach. Don't do it. It never helps, never. Kids need to learn to fight their own battles- to become their own advocates. I'm sure you are aware that once they turn 18, they are legal adults. If they go to college, you never see their grades or their health records without a waiver. You can't hold back time, so you might as well be prepared. Again, I'm not suggesting "hands-off." I'm suggesting "ears open."

I'll end with one of my favorite Irish proverbs:

"You've got to do

your own growing

No matter how tall your

grandfather was."

---

8 Takeaways from Yogi for Parents

1. Sports should be fun.
2. Kids should play more than one sport.
3. Give the games to the kids – we had our turn.
4. Support the coach – it's a hard job.
5. Stress hard work – nobody ever drowned in their own sweat.
6. Be your kid's biggest fan – always be positive.
7. Respect the game and the opponent.
8. Help less fortunate people.

8 Suggested Readings:

1. *A Revolution in the Bleachers* – Regan McMahon
2. *Reforming Sports Before the Clock Runs Out* – Bruce Svare
3. *Parenting Youth Athletes the Ripken Way* – Cal Ripken
4. *Mindset* – Carol Dweck
5. *101 Ways to be a Terrific Sports Parent* – Joel Fish with Susan Magee
6. *Just Let the Kids Play: How to Stop Other Adults From Ruining Your Child's Fun and Success in Youth Sport* – Bob Bigelow
7. *You Are NOT Special* – David McCullough Jr.
8. *Outliers* – Malcolm Gladwell

8 Suggested Videos:

1. *Friday Night Tykes* (Esquire Channel on YouTube)

2. *Philly Fan Catches Foul Ball; Gives it to Daughter* (YouTube)

3. *Trophy Kids* (HBO Productions)

4. *Promoting a Positive Athletic Experience: The Parent's Guide* (DVD)

5. *7 Tips for Parents of Athletes* (Teen Life DVD)

6. *What Makes a Nightmare Sports Parent – And what Makes a Great One?* (DVD)

7. *Steve Jobs Talks to Stanford Graduates* (Motivational Video – DVD)

8. *Dick and Rick Hoyt* (YouTube)

Note to parents

The larger part of this book is directed to you because I believe you are the most important mediator in negotiating the COMMON GROUND necessary for a successful athletic experience. There has been a lot of criticism directed your way recently, and I hope you don't feel like I am piling on. I really do understand that it's not easy being a sports parent. My primary goal is to inform you of what your youngsters and their coaches tell me that they want from you. Yogi's experiences, as well as mine, will hopefully provide you some guidelines for negotiating the ever-evolving landscape of youth sports. I suggest that you maintain an ongoing relationship with coaches and school guidance counselors in order to find realistic opportunities for your youngsters which will allow you to direct them on a path for personal as well as athletic growth.

If you skipped the first two parts, like I probably would have, in order to get to the material most relevant to you, please go back and read the information and suggestions offered to athletes and coaches. As I said in the Introduction, the only way to optimize the benefits of youth sports is to find common ground among the three participating parties: Athletes, Coaches, and Parents.

As parents, our major job is to be our kid's biggest fan. If our kid is the best player on the team, that doesn't mean we're a good parent. If our kid rarely plays, that doesn't mean we're a bad parent. It's not about us at all.

Appendix

NCAA Division I and II Athletic Scholarships

Sport	Full Scholarships Available	Full & Partial Scholarships Awarded	Dollar Amount	Average Received
Division I				
Baseball	2,956.10	8,064.70	71,118,600	8,818
Men's Basketball	4,046.70	4,244.10	118,834,800	28,000
Women's Basketball	4,329.60	4592	122,737,600	26,728
Football	15,977.20	18,596.80	415,902,800	22,364
Men's Soccer	1,683.00	3,702.60	50,688,000	13,689
Women's Soccer	3,591.90	6,723.30	93,635,000	13,962
Softball	2,774.40	4,569.60	68,652,800	15,023
Division II				
Baseball	1,425.00	5,650.00	26,850,000	4,852
Men's Basketball	2,314.70	3,779.70	49,048,200	12,976
Women's Basketball	2,205.00	3,851.40	45,687,600	11,862
Football	4,024.80	10,779.60	70,886,400	6,575
Men's Soccer	996.8	3115	21,039,600	6,754
Women's Soccer	1,271.20	4,131.40	25,128,900	6,082
Softball	1251.2	3,998.40	23,718,400	5,931

Source: NCAA

What are the Odds?

Estimated probability of competing in athletics beyond the high school interscholastic level:

	Men's Basketball	Women's Basketball	Football	Baseball	Men's Ice Hockey	Men's Soccer
High School Athletes	545,145	444,809	1,112,303	473,184	37,255	383,824
NCAA Athletes	16,911	15,381	64,879	29,816	4,101	21,601
Athletes Drafted by the Pros	44	32	250	600	33	76
The Odds of Getting There						
High School to NCAA	3.10%	3.50%	5.80%	6.30%	11.00%	5.60%
NCAA to Pros	1.20%	0.90%	1.70%	9.10%	3.60%	1.60%
High School to Pros	0.03%	0.03%	0.08%	0.44%	0.31%	0.07%

Note: These percentages are based on estimated data.
Source: NCAA

The best way to determine whether or not your son/daughter is an "elite" athlete is by looking at who is recruiting him/her. There are no secrets in Division I. A Hall of Fame major league coach once said, "If a kid can hit, we'll find him in a closet."

The percentage of athletes who receive a scholarship to a Division I school:

1.4%   Football

0.4%   Boys Soccer

1.0%   Girls Soccer

0.9%   Girls Cross Country/Track and Field

0.5%   Boys Cross Country/Track and Field

0.7%   Boys Basketball

0.9%   Girls Basketball

0.6%   Baseball

0.7%   Softball

0.3%   Wrestling

0.8%   Boys Swimming and Diving

1.2%   Girls Swimming and Diving

0.6%   Boys Tennis

1.1%   Girls Tennis

0.6%   Boys Golf

1.6%   Girls Golf

Source: NCAA

Moms and Dads Swept up in a "Not so Amazing Race"

The Star Ledger, 2013

By John D. McCarthy

"What does your kid want?" is always my first question to a parent. That's exactly what I said to a woman who called me after my op-ed, "Parents in the Bleachers, Bite Your Lip," appeared in the *Star-Ledger*. She identified herself as a writer, married to a journalist, and the mother of a seven-year-old daughter who has recently entered the world of youth sports.

She prefaced her questions saying that she and her husband were definitely not those over-the-top parents who micromanage their daughter's life. She sounded frazzled; her tale quickly struck a familiar chord.

New to the town and the local sports scene, she was hoping her daughter could have fun while learning soccer in a recreational league. Unfortunately, she was informed that the rec program had been dropped because parents were more interested in a "competitive experience" for their future Mia Hamms. She also learned that while all of the parents were vocal in their support for a travel team, none were willing to serve as a coach. "Before I knew it, my husband and I were sucked into coaching the team. What a disaster that turned out to be!

"The kids were great, but the parents were ridiculous. They constantly screamed instructions from the sidelines, abused the referees, many of whom were high school age, and regularly complained to my husband about playing time. Can you believe it?" she asked. Regrettably, I can. Accelerating athletic development is merely the latest trend in Americans' obsessive desire to be first and best, regardless of the cost.

Ralph Waldo Emerson cautioned Americans that, while advancement is a good thing, the rate must be consistently monitored or, "We will not ride the railroad, it will ride us." Many parents now feel that the train carrying young athletes is rolling by them at an Acela-like pace, and if their kids don't hop on board they'll be left behind.

The evidence is all around us. Neighborhood teams have been replaced by travel and elite squads. Dad's backyard tosses have been handed over to a pitching coach. The all-around, three-sport athlete has become a dinosaur, replaced by the 12 month specialist. High school coaches are becoming irrelevant; it's the AAU coach who now matters. Parents are shelling out thousands of dollars for equipment, private instruction, showcases, and sports psychologists' fees, and for what? The less than 1% chance of a professional career in sports? The slim hope of a college scholarship?

According to the NCAA, of 900,000 high school football players each year, only 6% will make a college team, and of that number, only 2% will be drafted into the NFL. The figures are roughly the same in basketball, and these are the only sports where each team member is awarded a scholarship. In Division I, only nine soccer, 11 volleyball, and 11 baseball scholarships are available for the entire team. Additionally, and contrary to popular belief, there is no such thing as a "full-ride." A scholarship is for one year only and must be renewed. True, most are, but none are guaranteed, and the number of college athletes who give back their scholarships each year continues to grow, prompting one frustrated athlete to write, "It's Not an Adventure. It's a Job."

To be good at anything requires passion and practice. Without the passion, an athlete isn't likely to put in the hours required to master a sport. While the single most important factor necessary for success at the highest level of sports might be talent, practice can certainly help an athlete get better, and help him or her reach full potential. It's our kid's passion and willingness to put the time into practice that matters, not ours.

I often hear parents say, "My kid is the best; he just needs to be noticed." Meanwhile, I hear coaches say all the time, "There are no secrets in Division I. We don't miss anyone." As Sparky Anderson, a highly successful major league manager once said, "If a kid can hit, we'll find him in a closet." Of course, as parents we are supposed to think our kid is great – a great <u>kid</u>! A great kid who happens to play a sport – a sport that reflects his interest and ability, but does not define him. When the focus of sports participation is getting a scholarship, the pressure on the athlete becomes enormous, and as parents, our tunnel vision causes us to lose our perspective. Then *we* become the over-the-top parents other parents whisper about. Our kids are likely to be among the 75% of kids who give up on sports before they're 13. Before reaching that point, we need to step back and look at the big picture.

A rational look at the risk-reward ratio would lead even the most speculative investor among us to consider the following NCAA release: There are $1 billion in athletic scholarships available each year. There are $22 billion in academic scholarships. Do the math. Is it worth investing our money in private coaching, travel teams, and showcases when the statistics show that the possibility of winning a scholarship is so minimal while the reality is that we will lose countless hours at home with the entire family, including those that aren't interested in sports. That's a question we need to answer before we check into some motel in a city or state we'd never travel to by choice for a weekend tournament.

As parents we can't just say, "We got caught up in the momentum," or that "We got sucked into the process," of accelerating kids into the current sports culture. No one has a gun to our heads. We shouldn't abrogate our responsibility to decide what's best for our children. We can, and must, reexamine the direction in which others are seducing us to follow. Before we know it, as a buddy of mine said, "ESPN will be conducting the embryonic draft!"

We know that sports can teach our kids many valuable lessons. What do they learn from seeing us disparage and belittle referees, berate and badger coaches, insist on providing our post-game analysis? All because we don't want anyone to derail their ride to elite sports status?

When I give a talk to high school athletes, and I have given hundreds, I always ask them, "What do you want from sports?" Usually they respond, "To be able to compete," "To have fun with my friends," or "To just fit in at school." When I ask them, "What do you want from your parents?" they say, "To support me; to let me make my own decisions; and most of all, to stop pressuring me and my coach." THAT is what most kids want.

"You're Perfectly Entitled to Think It – Just Don't Say It!"

The Star Ledger, March 2009

By John D. McCarthy

A PARENT'S SURVIVAL GUIDE
FOR WATCHING YOUTH SPORTS

Soon this year's crop of teen and pre-teen athletes will appear on a myriad of playing surfaces. Shaking off months of muscular lethargy, they'll be put through their paces, just like their professional counterparts, in the annual ritual of pre-season training. But what about you, their most ardent, sometimes too passionate supporters? Their Gatorade-lugging, unpaid-chauffeuring, ego-massaging parents? If you're one of those parents who has screamed so loud at an umpire that you became lightheaded and nearly passed out, or someone whose face turned beet red from anger or embarrassment after being asked to vacate the playing area, either your heart is going to explode or your spouse is going to kill you. Don't despair. You're not doomed, you're not a fanatic, and most importantly, you're not alone. Maybe it's time for you to limber up with some mental calisthenics.

Mike Bloomberg admits that he gets more nervous watching his daughter compete as an equestrian than he does running the most challenging city in the world. I know you can relate to New York City's even-tempered mayor. You don't watch "kids play games." You watch your flesh and blood, your DNA, your only link to immortality, struggle in a life and death battle. That's your free throw, your triple, your game-winning goal.

How are you expected to sit calmly at a game, as though you're at a lecture on the ways meditation can lower blood pressure? Be serious. Well, maybe not serious, but let's try practical. Humor me while I ask you a few questions:

- When you yell, and/or curse, at game officials, what are you hoping to accomplish? To get the ref or ump to realize the error of their ways and make calls favoring the team you came to root for? Think about some of your tired phrases: "Open your eyes, ref, you're missing a good game," "You're the worst ump I've ever seen," "Why don't you go back to Foot Locker?" Do these phrases have even a scintilla of a chance of currying favor? You know they don't. In fact, your own experience should tell you that game officials NEVER, and I mean, NEVER, appreciate these disparaging comments. If your goal is to help your son's or daughter's team, your remarks will surely guarantee the opposite result. *Think what you want, just don't say it!*

- When you constantly challenge a coach's competence and judgment at a volume that needs no technical amplification, what are you hoping to accomplish? To get the coach to agree with you, especially after you berated him or her from the opening pitch or whistle to the final batter or buzzer, all within earshot of his/her family and friends? You have as much chance of that happening as you do of being asked to sit on the bench as the "guest coach" for the next game. Again, count to ten, take a walk, text yourself– *Think what you want, just don't say it.*

- When you confront your kid's coach on the phone, or as he or she is exiting the playing area, demanding to know why your kid didn't play, or didn't play enough, what are you hoping to accomplish? To have the coach admit that you're right and promise to increase minutes, maybe even start your kid? My experience is that your kid will be buried on the bench longer than Cubs fans have waited for a World Series title. Will that be fair? No, but it's unquestionably going to happen. In my 40 years of following high school and college sports, I have NEVER, and I mean NEVER, seen or heard of a coach who increased a player's minutes after being challenged by an irate parent. Again, breathe deeply, recite the Serenity Prayer, stroll to your car. *Think what you want, just don't say it.*

Here's the bottom line. You may be a very astute sports fan with an eye for talent and a thorough knowledge of the rules. The fact is, you sit in the stands, not on the bench, and you don't get to make substitutions. You might be correct about a call, but the fact is you stand in the bleachers, not on the court, or on the field, and your calls don't count. As much as you love your offspring and want his/her team to be victorious, there is absolutely nothing you can do to affect the outcome. Why not sit back and let your kid compete without your inserting yourself into the equation? I'm lousy at math, but even I can see that your unsolicited, unappreciated opinions don't add up to any favorable outcome for your child. No one is asking you to give up your love of sports, or to become indifferent to your child's participation, and it's not only arrogant but ridiculous to tell you what to think. Your kid needs you to be a supporter, not an advocate. My suggestion? Bite your lip. You'll save face, and who knows, maybe a life, yours. That will make your kid very happy.

How To Tell If You're An "Over The-Top" Sports Parent

Rob Gilbert, Ph.D.

*Department of Exercise Science and Physical Education
Montclair State University*

How do you know when you go too far as a sports parent? What's really "over the top?" It's interesting that what we can instantly spot in other parents, we rarely see in ourselves.

Here's a check-list to see if you're in denial: Check off all the items that apply to you. There will be a scoring key at the end.

1. You use the word "we" when referring to your child's team.
2. You cheer and applaud only for your child.
3. You try hard to be the coach's best friend.
4. You know the referees and umpires by their first names.
5. The referees and umpires know you by sight and reputation.
6. The athletic director sits close to you during games.
7. You use a stopwatch to keep track of exactly how much playing time your child gets.
8. Your cars and mini-vans sport numerous bumper stickers with school logos.
9. You have a bumper sticker that reads: "My soccer player is an honor student."
10. While in the stands, you keep statistics (like batting averages) and you update them throughout the game.
11. You keep stats on every member of the team.
12. You wear your child's team or school paraphernalia from head to toe.
13. You dress this way even on days when there isn't a game.

14. You make sure your parents (the grandparents) wear the appropriate paraphernalia.

15. Your young children, and even the infants, wear the team paraphernalia.

16. You know the players on the opposing team by name.

17. You know their parents.

18. You know all the websites where there may be coverage of your child's team.

19. You scout upcoming opponents.

20. You use a stopwatch during a soccer games to keep track of the time. When necessary, you correct the referees.

21. You have your kids "held back" in school so they can repeat a grade for an athletic advantage.

22. You sell your home and move to another town to play for a certain coach.

23. You complain that the local paper doesn't cover youth sports enough.

24. You come out of the stands and cheer right alongside the cheerleaders.

25. You have a video-archive of footage for every moment your child has ever played.

26. You have a newspaper-archive for every sports-related reference to your child.

27. You miss work to attend practices and you're not even a coach!

28. You make cardboard signs for every game.

29. You have signs professionally made.

30. You own a rule book and take it to games… just in case.

SCORING KEY: If you've checked more than one of the items above—you are officially "over-the-top."

REMEMBER: The games belong to the kids, not their parents.

Rob Gilbert has taught sport psychology for 30 years at Montclair State University and is the co-founder of the Institute for Coaching and Sports Parenting at the Yogi Berra Museum.

GOOD SPORTSMANSHIP – OVERRATED?

"C'mon, Johnny, be a good sport, someone has to lose."

By John D. McCarthy

Don't get me wrong, I'm not a fan of boorish behavior on the part of athletes, coaches, or spectators. It's just that I have no faith in "feel good – Pollyanna" appeals to people's better nature to act civilly toward one another in the heat of athletic competition. Our culture isn't currently capable of cultivating "good losers." We're not wired that way. Our culture venerates winners and ridicules losers. Is it any wonder then that helmets are thrown, water coolers are overturned, rival fans are taunted or jeered, umpires are cursed at, or in increasing instances, assaulted? Is it any wonder then that athletes, coaches, and parents act like narcissistic children with an over-inflated sense of entitlement, or that they rationalize aberrant behavior as a by-product of athletic competition? The answer is a resounding NO! While it isn't possible to change culture as a whole, it is most certainly possible to change the culture of sports. A solution to poor sportsmanship that permeates much of today's sports landscape is much easier to arrive at than one might think, and surprisingly, it doesn't call for a de-emphasis on winning.

Winning Matters

Having been involved in sports most of my life, I am totally convinced that any attempt to improve sportsmanship by de-emphasizing winning is doomed to failure. Ever since the colonists won their freedom from England, winning has been a staple in America's ethos. The celebrations after victories in both world wars were ever-present in the first newsreels Baby Boomers ever saw. A loss, even a perceived loss like in Vietnam, has consequences which last decades. The very nature of any conflict suggests there will be a winner and a loser, and while we're reluctant to admit it, there are parallels between sports and war, even in the terminology ("to the victors go the spoils," "in the heat of the battle," "an aerial assault"). It would be great if we played competitive sports for their pure enjoyment, but that time has long past. Once a tournament begins, the emotion and the desire to win is the same for the athletes, coaches, and parents, whether it's the NCAA Final Four or the New Jersey under 12 travel team.

It amazes me that two of the winningest coaches in the history of sports in America, Vince Lombardi and John Wooden, have shared their approach for athletic success in countless interviews and in print and we still don't get it. These two icons prepared their teams to play against the game, regardless of the opponent. Both were teachers who enjoyed practice more than the games. Neither had to lecture their players about sportsmanship. Their players were taught to respect the game and that led naturally to respect for their opponent. Were they any less jubilant when they were victorious because they beat the game instead of their archrival? Hardly. Watch their championship videos and see for yourself.

Changing the focus in athletic competition to beating the game, instead of trouncing the opponent, doesn't diminish "The Thrill of Victory." It merely shifts the emphasis from the outcome to the preparation. Most sports fans embrace the most famous axiom in sports, attributed to the legendary coach of the Green Bay Packers, Vince Lombardi, that "winning isn't everything, it's the only thing." Problem is, Lombardi never said that. What he said was, "The will to win is not as important as the will to prepare." Lombardi's teams ran very few offensive plays. His focus was on the execution of those few plays. What separated him from the other coaches was his ability to motivate his players to commit themselves to practice the fundamentals over and over until they achieved mastery. The Packers didn't care who lined up against them. If they played like they practiced, they'd win, and win they did, including the first two Super Bowls.

A Dose of Realism

First, let's agree that mandating a code of behavior doesn't guarantee compliance. If that were possible, there would be no jails. Secondly, let's agree that getting athletes to compete with character can't be accomplished merely by using buzz words or catchy slogans. Nancy Reagan tried to dissuade teens from using drugs with the slogan: "Just Say No!" How'd that work out? Quotes are wonderful; they're thought-provoking, insightful, and uplifting. However, they rarely produce a significant change in behavior. What's needed instead is a specific, achievable action plan that doesn't deprive us of the things we cherish: training to compete, testing our resolve, and experiencing triumph. What's needed instead of buzz words is a simple strategy, and here it is: Instead of ramping up athletes to vanquish their opponents, teach them to PLAY AGAINST THE GAME. In doing so, we might elevate sports to an art form, similar to a dance, and the opponent, instead of being regarded as the enemy, becomes a partner in the dance. Interestingly the goal of every Division I basketball player is to make it to the NCAA tournament, a magical three-week athletic carnival that captivates the nation's imagination, a tournament referred to as "The Big Dance."

The True Test

To evaluate the strategy I have offered, we need to put it to a test encompassing the realm of sports participation, from tee-ball to the Super Bowl. Watch any novice to a sport. He has all he can do to swing a bat without getting hit in the head, cradle a ball and heave it an ungodly distance into a hoop, or get into a stance without having his chinstrap get trapped inside of his shoulder pads. Of course, he's wearing a new uniform, and a bunch of kids have on a different colored uniform. He doesn't really know, or care, what team he is on. He can't even read his jersey, and wouldn't know what a Titan is anyway. He can't be concerned with anyone in a different colored jersey.

What exactly is an opponent anyway? He has no idea. He has all he can do not to hurt himself. An exaggeration? For sure, but the point is, we start out in sports trying to understand our body and our movements. Then we learn the fundamentals, whether it's tackling, shooting, hitting, or skating. Our earliest sense of self-worth comes from the gradual mastery of these fundamentals and from gaining an understanding of the rules of the game.

Someone else, our coaches or our parents, tells us about THE NEED TO DEFEAT THE OPPOSITION! We just love the action; everything else, winning, being the best, etc., becomes interference. Think not? Then why do 75% of kids stop playing sports by the age of 13? Sure, there are a number of reasons, such as other interests or talents, etc., but the number one answer given by kids who stopped playing was, "It wasn't fun anymore."

Fast-forward to the Super Bowl between the Patriots and the Giants in 2008. Except for the Giants themselves, and their most die-hard supporters, everyone knew the Patriots were a prohibitive favorite. Everyone that is except perhaps legendary UCLA basketball coach, John Wooden. When asked, which team wins the big games? Wooden replied, "The best team doesn't win; the team that plays the best wins. The team that plays closest to how it practices wins." Translation: The team THAT BEATS THE GAME WINS. Many people would argue that the team with the best players wins. Really? The Patriots had 11 All-Pro selections, the Giants had one. Others would argue that the team that wants it most wins. Really? The Patriots weren't hell-bent on becoming the first team to go undefeated and win the Super Bowl since the '72 Dolphins? The Patriots weren't ready to give it their all to become the first 19-0 team and be regarded as perhaps the best team of all time? What happened was the Giants out-executed the Patriots that day. They played the game better than the Patriots played the game that day.

Under Control

In sports, just as in life, there's a limit to what one can control. Athletes can't actually "control" their opponents, and they most certainly can't "control" game officials. What they can control is their preparation, concentration, emotion, and execution. Dr. Rob Gilbert, a sports psychologist from Montclair State University, offers the following formula for success: $P = P - I$. One's Performance equals one's Potential, minus Interference. His theory purports the idea that the success of an athlete is equal to his ability to execute his plan while factoring out all interference. Interference can be internal ("I must win," "I need a scholarship," "People are watching me," etc.), or external ("I'm videotaping your game today, son," "If you can't do the job, we'll get someone else," "Hey, #12, you stink!" etc.). According to the theory then, the athlete who can eliminate the interference ("noise") has the better chance of being successful.

Think of all the times you've heard coaches or players say after a loss: "The pressure got to us;" "We weren't focused;" "We just didn't shoot/tackle/pitch well." What they're actually saying is they didn't execute the fundamentals; they didn't BEAT THE GAME. Games are often decided by a shot that hits the bar, a double fault, a missed free throw, or an error. What does an opponent have to do with these specific failures to execute? Nothing. Unless of course the athlete paid more attention to the opponent than to the performance of an action he has successfully completed hundreds of times during practice.

Competitive Character

By now you might agree that an athlete's success rate can improve by focusing on controlling the things he can control, but you may be wondering what that has to do with sportsmanship. Plenty. If coaches focus more on how to beat the game than on why they need to beat this particular team; if athletes focus on doing what they have practiced rather than the ranking of the team they're facing, then it's more likely that their focus will change to what they need to do in order to win, instead of needing to beat a cross-town rival. That kind of pressure adversely impacts individual performance. Also, if players learn to focus solely on what they can control, it will be easier to comport themselves appropriately during the game and in post-game situations. They might even understand better what it takes to beat the game, and therefore respect those who have done so. Post-game handshakes might become more genuine. Right now they're perfunctory.

The game of golf is a perfect example of competing with the correct perspective. It's a given that professional golfers are always aware of Tiger Woods' presence, but still they remain focused on beating the course. Their goal is to beat par. They can't control Tiger's scorecard; they can only control their own. No one understands that better than Tiger. Remember his dramatic victory for the 2008 U.S. Open title? After four rounds and a Monday playoff of 19 holes against Rocco Mediate with the largest viewing audience ever, Tiger finished 1 under. That's why he practices harder than anyone to beat the game, and that's why he is so highly respected by his peers. Peers, by the way, who respect the game so much that they add strokes to their scorecard for rules infractions that, in most instances, go unnoticed by others. While it's true that golf isn't a contact sport, it has lessons to teach all athletes. Golfers accept that their fate is in their hands. They don't make excuses. They don't talk trash, and most importantly, their respect for their game is unwavering.

"Noise" Factors

No discussion about sportsmanship would be complete without addressing the role of parents and spectators. There's probably not much that is harder to do for a parent, relatively speaking, than to watch an offspring participate in a game, particularly a conference or state championship. They worry about injury, embarrassment, and defeat. Guess what?

These possible outcomes are beyond their control. They might be able to prevent their child from dropping his baby brother, but they can't prevent him from dropping a pop fly.

Parents need to be mindful that the players on the opposing team have parents who are experiencing the same anguish they are. So why are they shouting, "Miss it, Drop it," etc.? The primary role of parents, and basically their only role, is to be their child's biggest supporter. If they can't control their nerves, they should try rooting for the entire team, not just their kid. Many parents tell how being less singularly focused alleviates some of their stress. Other parents suggest taking their own "time-out" by going for a walk when their anxiety is getting the better of them.

If parents really want to be helpful, they need to minimize the "noise" their youngsters have to deal with during a game. Parents need to stop yelling. They need to stop yelling instructions to their youngster while he is trying to perform. Parental yelling can change the players' focus from what they can control to what they can't. They also need to stop yelling at coaches and game officials. It sets a bad example, and it's never helpful. The more time they spend venting their anger at umpires and referees, the less focused they are on what really determines the outcome of the game, the execution of fundamentals by the players. Furthermore, parents who feel they can influence game officials are delusional. I've yet to see a call reversed by an official simply because someone yelled, "Open your eyes, you're missing a good game!"

Parental "noise" impacts on their athletes more than they might realize. A recent Stanford University study pointed out that 85% of young athletes identify the PGA (Post Game Analysis) by parents as the thing they like least about playing sports. The expectation that their performance, and that of the coaches and game officials, is going to be critiqued on the ride home and frequently dissected with the aid of videotape creates a level of apprehension that undoubtedly creeps into the player's psyche during the game.

Finally, a word about spectators in general. It has become all too common to witness "fans" cross the line from observers to participants. They taunt opposing players, berate officials, verbally challenge coaches, storm the playing surface, and on occasion, physically assault opposing fans. My unscientific belief is that these unacceptable behaviors are generally exhibited by those individuals who have never played, or have never had any success playing sports. Those who can't relate to the time and energy it takes to master an athletic skill. It takes years. Those who believe that their paid admission allows them to do or say whatever they want. It does not. Those who believe they're part of the event. They are not. Students demonstrating school spirit, or residents exhibiting town pride, are admirable. Their thunderous applause is a welcomed part of an athletic event, just as it is with any performance, say the "Big Dance."

Fans can and should support their teams without becoming derisive. If they don't learn to control their frustration and anger, games will be played without spectators present. In some cities, they already are. That's not the answer. Athletic events are meant to be fun for everyone. However, the only action that matters occurs on the playing surface, not in the bleachers.

Truth Is...

I love sports. They've been a major part of my life, as a player, a coach, and currently as a college instructor in sports psychology. At times I worry that we've lost our way, but then I see players, coaches, parents, and athletic directors who do "get it." They understand that a game determines which team played better on a given day, and that's all. The result of a game has an impact on them, but it doesn't define them. The uniforms will change as well as the venue, but the game will still be the same. It may beat them today, but it's not the end of their world. As Charles Schultz noted, "It's already tomorrow in Australia." So let's keep on competing, and let's keep on dancing.

Acknowledgements

This book wouldn't exist without the graciousness of Yogi and his family. Their trust in my ability to accurately portray Yogi as a model for athletes, coaches and parents guided my conscience throughout the process. Thank you Yogi, Carmen, Larry, Timmy, and especially Dale, who generously gave his time to previewing the book and writing the foreword. Yogi is the most decent man I have ever met. I hope my work does justice to his legacy.

Dave Kaplan, YBM Director, was the one who informed me that the mission of the Museum, and thereby The Coaching Institute and Center for Sports Parenting at the YBM, is to preserve the legacy of a man who became an American icon for who he is as much as for what he accomplished as a Hall of Fame baseball player. Thanks Dave for giving me the opportunity to share your vision and for providing me with anecdotes from Yogi's illustrious career.

In Catholic school, I learned that theft is a sin. For stealing many ideas from my friend and colleague, Rob Gilbert, I confess my guilt. Without his generosity I would not have been able to enjoy my 'Second Act' as an adjunct professor at Montclair State, and I wouldn't have been able to sprinkle in helpful suggestions throughout this book. If you don't like the book, blame him. He made me write it.

There are innumerable ideas interspersed in the text that I learned about from coaches with whom I have worked, most notably: Russ Monica, Matty Lombardi, Ollie Gelston, Mike Cohen and Fred Hill, Jr.

I also need to thank coaches who have given me access to their teams, and shown me the way good coaches become significant. Included among them are Ted Jarmusz, John Ziemba,

Ken Trimmer, John Fiore, Doug Nevins, Mike Tully, Stephan Zichella, Elliot Lovi, Mike Sheppard, Jr., Ted Fiore, Rick Giancola, Rich O'Connor, Lorenzo Sozio, Rob O'Connor, Todd Smith, Bianca Brown, Greg Tynes and Paul Raiz.

Support from athletic directors has significantly aided our work at the Museum and provided me with an opportunity to share Yogi's outlook on youth sports with hundreds of student/athletes. Many thanks to John Porcelli, Todd Smith, Damion Macioci, Rich Porfido, Gary Farishian, Tom D'Elia, Pat Genova, Dr. Ted D'Alessio, Joe Piro, Gus Kalinkas, Jeff Gannon, Injoo Han, Tony DeOrio, Lorenzo Sozio, Larry Buschio, Steve Jenkins and the AD's from the Super Essex Conference who assist us in recognizing the Best Teammates each spring.

None of the efforts of the Coaching Institute would be possible without the funding from Investors Bank and their remarkable CEO, Kevin Cummings. His vision of sports 'done right' mirrors Yogi's, as does his humility.

Special thanks to Stephen Swinton of Swinton Design Studio for his assistance in formatting my manuscript for publication. His creativity and patience were invaluable. Thanks to Great Uncle Skippy, Mickey, and Alvaro Mangiacavallo for reading the initial draft.

On a personal level, I need to thank the people who have always been in my corner and supported me unconditionally: Pete DeSimone, Ed Morneau, Ken Bernabe, John Burns, Mark DiIonno, John Priori, Roy Innocenti, Maria Damiano, Kathie Grotto, Rich Eidman, Elliott Kalb, Eddie Dolan, my brother Kevin, my sister Noreen, and most of all my late brother Dennis, who was always my biggest fan. Their friendship and encouragement mean everything to me.

Finally, to the women in my life. To my daughter Erin, thanks for allowing me to share "our" story. Your welfare will always be my primary concern. To my wife, Poms, thanks for typing my handwritten draft (that's how old school I am!), for editing, and most of all, for your willingness to share history with me.

CPSIA information can be obtained
at www.ICGtesting.com
Printed in the USA
BVOW06*2054020217

475013BV00004B/4/P